SPANISH COLONIAL FURNITURE

Old Spanish chest with geometric carved design, the usual heavy lock, and strap-iron corner reinforcements

An old Spanish bench with shaped slats and mortise-and-tenon joints

SPANISH COLONIAL FURNITURE

A. D. WILLIAMS

SUNSTONE PRESS
SANTA FE

© 2019 by Sunstone Press
All Rights Reserved
No part of this book may be reproduced in any form or by any electronic or mechanical means including information storage and retrieval systems without permission in writing from the publisher, except by a reviewer who may quote brief passages in a review.

Sunstone books may be purchased for educational, business, or sales promotional use.
For information please write: Special Markets Department, Sunstone Press,
P.O. Box 2321, Santa Fe, New Mexico 87504-2321.

WWW.SUNSTONEPRESS.COM
SUNSTONE PRESS / POST OFFICE BOX 2321 / SANTA FE, NM 87504-2321 /USA
(505) 988-4418 / ORDERS ONLY (800) 243-5644 / FAX (505) 988-1025

Preface

This book is the outgrowth of some years of study of Spanish-American colonial furniture as this was developed in the vast territory now embraced in the states of Texas, Arizona, and New Mexico. The collection is offered in the hope that the designs which are frankly adaptations or copies of early pieces in private possession or preserved in museums, will appeal to homecraftsmen and students.

In the course of his career as a teacher in public schools and in Indian schools in the Southwest, the author at first followed the conventional plan of teaching the usual simple woodwork and furniture construction. Hardwoods were used and pieces of interest to students or of value to the schools and institutions were made. Little attention was given to the local inheritance of Spanish and Indian culture, until one day a very old Spanish colonial chest was brought into the school shop for repair. The excellent results of this simple job led to the study of locally available ancient pieces, and a number of tables and chairs were copied or adapted. Further study of old furniture and experiments in the school shops led to the gradual development of a course which has been successfully offered in grades seven to twelve.

The pieces developed have given satisfaction in the making and in daily use in the home and school, and are here offered in the hope that they will help perpetuate some of the valuable early American culture which has been long neglected.

The author expresses his hearty thanks to Mrs. F. J. Mathews, Las Vegas, New Mexico, for the illustrations of the chair with shaped slats, top of page 3, the chest at the bottom of page 4, and the cabinets on page 6; to Mr. J. H. Mathews, Albuquerque, New Mexico, for the illustration of the chest at the top of page 4.

THE AUTHOR

A fine old Spanish chest, highly carved, with heavy iron lock and corner reinforcements. Chest was brought in from Old Mexico and is now in the Hugh Caulkin's home in Old Town, New Mexico

Contents

Preface	v
I. Design and Construction	1
II. Practical Details of Design and Finish	8
Serving Tray	17
Smoking Stand	19
Wastepaper Box	21
Hall Tree	23
Sentinel Bookcase	25
Open Bookcase	27
Bookcase	29
Dining Chair	31
Dining Chair	33
Spanish Armchair	35
Spanish Armchair	37
Armchair	39
Armchair	41
Armchair	43
Coffee Table	45
End Table	47
End Table	49
End Table	51
Console Table	53
Square Table	55
Bedside Table	57
Living-Room Table	59
Dining Table	61
Dining Table	63
Library Table	65
Library Table	67
Occasional Table	69
Smoking Stand	71
Magazine Table	73
Fireplace Bench	75
Fireplace Bench	77
Patio Bench	79
Patio Bench	81
Wood Box	83
Early Spanish Chest	85
Chest	87
Spanish Colonial Chest	89
Dictionary Stand	91
Dictionary Stand	93
Twin Beds	95
Double Bed	97
Highboy	99
Spanish Highboy	101
Spanish Lowboy	103
Small Desk	107
Chest of Drawers	109
Chest	111
Dressing Table and Stool	113
Writing Desk	115
Typewriter Desk	117
Filing Cabinet	119
Wardrobe	121
Cupboard	123
Cupboard	124
Wall Cabinet	127
Wall Cabinet	129
Buffet	131
Index	135

CHAPTER I

Design and Construction

It is noteworthy that the widely separated sections of the United States, first settled by Europeans, developed original and artistically valuable styles of furniture. These styles, while quite different in form and spirit, are being perpetuated as a part of the American art heritage and constitute distinctly characteristic additions to the furnishing of present-day homes.

In New England the Pilgrims, soon after their coming, began to satisfy their need for furniture by making rather austerely utilitarian pieces — chairs, tables, stools, chests. The easily obtained and readily worked white pine was most widely used, and the designs were largely based on the pieces brought from England.

In the vast and sun-parched Southwest, the early Spanish settlers and their Indian charges developed an interesting type of furniture made of the only widely available wood, pine. This furniture reflected the romantic exuberance of the pieces brought from Spain, but was soon modified in character and ornament by the aboriginal Indian craftsmen who used their own mystical art motifs. Perhaps the present interest in the Spanish colonial furniture would be more widespread if the lack of intelligence of American furniture manufacturers of fifty years ago had not destroyed all appreciation and love for it by the clumsy, heavy, arts-and-crafts productions labeled "mission style." An intelligent study of the authentic Spanish colonial furniture, now on display in a growing number of public museums of the Southwest and in a number of the restored mission churches, indicates that the furniture has hitherto unsuspected

A heavy Spanish colonial chest carved with geometric design

elements of romance and beauty which deserve to be widely used and enjoyed in the Spanish type of American home of the present day.

The elements of design common to all Spanish colonial furniture were based upon the pieces which the more wealthy pioneers imported from Old Spain. This furniture was brought by wagon train from Mexico City or from St. Louis and consisted of heavily carved and richly inlaid hardwood pieces. Many of the tables had roped legs and wrought-iron decorations so characteristic of these centuries. Every piece thus imported became a model to be copied by the few white craftsmen and their numerous native Indian helpers. The latter, while they had practically no furniture in their own homes, had a rich material culture, and soon added to the furniture which they made for their conquistadores the numerous symbolic and geometric designs with which their blankets, pottery, and other objects were so interestingly ornamented.

The Spanish colonial homes had an atmosphere of character and individuality which grew out of the simple culture and rigorous life of the people. The thick adobe walls with

Cabinet for storing dishes

their rounded corners and uneven walls, from the roof the projecting vigas, the iron rejas at the windows, the patio, the strings of chili peppers cutting vivid lines against the white clay walls, were all picturesque and strangely exotic. One would expect to find room interiors equally interesting and distinctive. There were very few pieces of furniture. In the kitchen were a grain box, a box for the firewood, a table, a chair or two, and a wall cabinet, or alacena, for storing the cooking utensils and dishes. The dining room had a large table with a heavy top, carved legs, and sometimes iron braces. More often wood stretchers were used to stiffen the frame of the table. The straight-backed chairs were rather rigid in appearance, and not always comfortable. As a rule the room also had one or more wall cabinets and one or more benches. The furniture of the rest of the house was scant. There were a few armchairs,

Chest with symbolic geometric design

Chair with shaped slats and reeded crosspieces

Chair with turned spindles and crosspieces with carved Navajo mountain symbol

a box, and perhaps a desk; in the bedrooms were beds and chests of drawers. The chests usually were simple and had a drop lid carved and ornamented with lock and hinges. The corners of the boxes and chests were of dovetail construction. The writing desk usually was a chest mounted upon legs, and the front was hinged so it would drop down on supports that pulled out from under the bottom, thus forming a table for writing. The inside was filled with numerous small drawers. The seats of the chairs were often made of rawhide with the hair left on. If the hair had been removed, the hide was cut in strips about an

Bench with diamond-shaped slats and reeded crosspieces

inch wide and woven in a checkered basketry weave for the seats.

The Spanish colonial furniture of the early times was made mostly of pine, and the usual piece was made of low-grade lumber. Planks were split from logs and hewn by hand to the desired size. The construction of the pieces necessarily was heavy to overcome the weakness of the material. The pieces had to be carved or fluted to offset their massive effect and still retain sufficient strength for long and rough use. The joints were through mortise and tenon, and, to insure against hard use, they were invariably pinned. No nails or screws were used. Deeply colored spots in the lumber were considered attractive, and a solid knot was admired.

The early designers and craftsmen were not slow to adapt to the furniture they made the intricate geometric and symbolic designs which they found in Navajo blankets, and the more conservative but readily carved decorative features of the Pueblo pottery. Pigments were used by the Indians in pleasing combinations, and the prevailing dull reds and blues were widely used in the furniture. Chip carving was quite often used on flat surfaces, and the reds and blues were alternated in the different elements of the design. On other pieces the flat surfaces were decorated in low relief. For such decorations different variations of the rosette were much in favor. Either the concave or the convex design was used.

Chest with convex rosette design

Chest with concave rosette design

SOME ELEMENTS OF DESIGN

To judge by the few original pieces available for study, the Spanish colonial furniture maker was not the best of craftsmen. Wealth did not grow in that dry and hot land, for the reason that the natural resources which the explorers hoped for did not exist. The craftsman was too busy fighting for a bare living to take much time for doing fine cabinetwork. The charm of design and ornament which is characteristic of the best pieces was the result of the romantic spirit of the Spanish workmen, the religious zeal of the Franciscan missionaries, and the patience and mysticism of the Indians.

The best elements of design were the rosette, the offset rail and stretcher, and the setup used on the tops of chairs and bench backs. These were probably all copied from the Indians.

The rosette was originally round or oval shaped, with a smooth surface. It represented the Navajo hogan, a home that was built of logs, poles, and mud, with a hole in the center for the smoke to escape. The silversmiths were the first to use the design for concho belts. Later the plain surface of the rosette was broken up into several units, and was copied in this form as a decorative feature of furniture. The Navajo silversmiths of today have subdivided it again by decorating the single units of the design.

The offset contours of the table and bench stretchers were copied from the pueblo. The outline of the pueblo home shows a series of offsets, sometimes irregular, but as a rule having a certain amount of symmetry. The setup used on the tops of the back legs of chairs probably originated at the same source, or it may have come from the symbol used by the Navajo to represent a mountain. This symbol consists of a series of steps. Many of the stretchers, rails, and aprons of the early Spanish colonial pieces have a series of irregular steps. These are very similar to the steps in Navajo rug patterns which are largely geometric.

The crude representation of flowers used

Old Spanish trastero with turned door spindles

Bench with reeded crosspieces and slats

on the early pieces are possibly Mexican in origin. None of them are well done. They were often simply hammered into the smooth surface of the softwood with a blunt tool. They do not seem to have been made in a conscious effort to improve the appearance of the articles, and it seems hardly advisable that they be reproduced as a part of the decorative scheme of the Spanish colonial furniture of the present.

ADAPTING THE STYLE TO PRESENT-DAY USE

It is a far cry from the original houses of the Spanish colonists to the Spanish-American homes of today. All of the original advantages of plan and even the adobe construction and the picturesque tile roofs have been retained, as have the projecting vigas and the rejas. But the whole exterior and interior have taken on a different tone. The homes now are spacious and cool, and have an atmosphere of repose and charm. Ease and comfort have taken the place of ruggedness so that rigid reproductions of the original furnishings would be inconsistent and impractical. There is no longer a need for the extreme heaviness of the old pieces. The uncomfortable straightness of the chairs and benches, the strap-iron reinforcements on the corners of chests, and the wooden pins holding the bed rails are wholly unnecessary and undesirable. The exuberance of the ornate carving of Old Mexico, and the excesses in the proportions of minor and major segments of the old pieces are distinctly out of place at present — appropriate and admired as these features were in the old pieces.

In designing and making the pieces illustrated and described in the present book, the best elements of design to be found in the Spanish colonial have been used as a foundation. To this have been added contemporary features distinctly Spanish, such

Old cabinet with turned stiles

Cupboard with variety of carving and heavy door hinges

as the roped leg, and symbols distinctly Indian, such as the rosette and the feather contour of stretcher and rail. These Indian symbols, used in pleasing combinations, have been found to give effects that are distinctive. They are more restful than the ornate carvings of Old Mexico. While the elements of decoration have been kept wherever possible, more geometric designs and Indian symbols are being used than will be found in the originals. Thus the dominant qualities of the old have been tempered with sufficient restraint, so that the articles made by the present-day craftsman will fit into our modern Spanish homes.

If the pieces suggested depart somewhat from the originals in line and ornament, they also involve necessary changes in structure. The through mortise-and-tenon joints are glued, but they are also pegged for decorative purposes. On tables, spiral legs, and wherever possible, twisted iron braces have been used. The back legs of the chairs have been strengthened by better proportion, and the whole chairs have been made more comfortable by more careful design.

Spanish-type architecture is perceptibly increasing. Although it suffered neglect and partial eclipse at one time, it has never died out in the Southwest, and at the present time

Old Spanish chest with crude carving and heavy lock. Found in Old Town, New Mexico. Stand is modern

Another old chest highly carved with geometric designs

it is dominant in the minds of architects and home builders. It has always existed in Florida and the South, and has now invaded the Midwest. The Spanish type of house interior calls for atmosphere and nothing can give this effect as well as a Spanish mode of interior decoration. The tone must be rather austere, positive, and imposing, yet tempered with comfort and ease. It may be luxurious, but it must maintain a simple dignity. It is felt that the different articles of furniture described in this text will fit into such a home. In fact, the demand has so increased that it bears out the validity of this assumption.

Chest with rosette and feather carving

CHAPTER II

Practical Details of Design and Finish

ROSETTES

In early Spanish-American period furniture the rosette probably was used as an ornament more than any other figure. Many variations of this figure now are used. Most rosettes in Spanish work have six units, or a multiple of six, so that the ornament can be laid out with a compass and dividers or triangles.

To locate the center of the rosette, construct the diagonals of the space. Using this center, describe a circle tangent to the space to be covered by the design. Divide the circle into quadrants by perpendicular and horizontal bisectors. Then, taking these four points of intersection, and with a radius equal to the radius of the original circle, swing arcs each way from these points of intersection to divide

Elliptical and round rosette carvings

Round and diamond-shaped rosette carvings

the circumference into twelve equal parts. Connect these points by lines through the center of the circle dividing the area. Construct smaller arcs to subtend the twelve divisions of the circumference, giving the figure the appearance of a flower.

Begin carving by cutting V-shaped grooves on all lines about $1/8$ inch deep near the center and $1/4$ inch deep near the circumference. Do not use too much pressure on the carving knife where the lines converge at the center. Carve away the surrounding area with a $1/2$-inch straight gouge, or, if the figure is small, use a smaller tool.

In the larger areas the design should stand out about $1/4$ inch in relief. It is best to do the carving before finishing the rosette as the gouge may slip and chip small pieces from the figure. When this surface has been carved, begin rounding the edges of the design with the heel of the carving knife or the skew chisel. Sand out all chisel or knife marks with fine sandpaper. This will result in a rounded convex surface showing the grain of the wood in smooth flowing curves.

For another form of the rosette, lay out the design the same as in the preceding paragraphs, but instead of making the surface convex, make it concave by the use of a gouge. In doing this the area outside the figure is left flat. These concave rosettes were possibly more popular than the first form. They are much less work, but they were seldom done well enough by the early craftsman to bring out the beauty of the grain of the wood.

Another form of the rosette in common use was that used on the doors of some of the wall cabinets. To make this design, lay out the rosette in a manner similar to that described in the beginning of this chapter. Broaden the lines to about ⅜ inch wide by drawing parallel lines on each side of the originals. Cut away the surrounding area with a gouge to the depth of about ⅛ inch, leaving the design in relief and with a flat surface. The surrounding surface is left with the gouge marks. Be sure to follow the grain of the wood, so that smooth cuts result.

Many variations of the rosette are used in the decorative features of Spanish colonial furniture. One half or two thirds of a rosette figure can be used to decorate the top of a bed or wall cabinet; the corners of a large area can be broken up with three or four units of the figure, or the horizontal portions of the figure can be used in a decorative scheme.

Quite often a portion of the rosette used is not an arc of a true circle. An elliptical curved portion on the headpiece of a bed might be decorated with units of the design in a regular scheme or pattern. The fan-shaped decorations used on the top of the wall cabinet or cupboard are often elongated at the base so that the outline of the top does not form an arc of a circle. These are possibly later variations that were invented to relieve monotonous repetition of the rosette based on the circle. The earlier decorations were conventional, limited, and did not show much ingenuity.

SPIRAL LEGS

The layout for carving the spiral legs of Spanish colonial furniture is not as complicated as it would seem.

First, cut the stock to the desired size and length. A spiral leg looks lighter than one which is not carved; it is, consequently, advisable to use a larger square than would be necessary ordinarily.

Second, lay off the dimensions at the top for rails and at the bottom for the feet. The rails can be any width desired, but the feet should be in proportion to the length and thickness of the square of the leg. A leg 4 inches square should have a foot 4½ or 5 inches high, while a leg 2 inches square should have a 3- or 3½-inch foot.

Third, after laying off the dimensions for the feet and rails, prepare to lay off the portion of the leg which is to be carved as a spiral. If the leg is 2 inches square, begin at the lower end of the stock immediately above the foot, and lay off 2-inch sections by running lines around the squares. If the leg is 2¾ inches square, lay off 2¾-inch sections, and in a similar manner handle legs of different sizes. After these parallel lines are run around the legs forming squares on each side, begin at the bottom and run one diagonal line across each square. These diagonals will make a continuous spiral line around the leg, traveling from bottom to top.

Fourth, on two of the legs have the spiral travel to the right as it goes up, and on the other two have it travel to the left. In this way, the spiral travels *out* on the front view of the piece of furniture and travels *in* on the end view. In the front view, the spiral on the left leg will travel clockwise and on the right leg it will move counterclockwise.

Fifth, set the marking gauge at 5/16 inch for the 2-inch square, and run lines from each of the corners on the two adjoining faces for the length of the spiral to be carved. This shows the depth to run the saw in cutting the groove for the spiral. With the 2¾-inch legs, and the 3-inch legs, set the gauge at ⅜ inch; and with the 4-inch legs, use a ½-inch dimension on the gauge. If the grooves and ridges are to run close together in the spiral, cut each of the diagonals to the depth indicated, but if the roping is to be farther apart, cut out every other diagonal. In this latter case, be sure to mark the spiral lines that are to be left, with a black crayon. The beginner is likely to saw the wrong lines unless they are well marked.

In most of the projects illustrated in this book every other diagonal is cut except in the short legs for the base of the chest of drawers. The instructions on each project clearly indicate whether the groove runs from each corner or every other corner. In general, a good rule to follow is to cut every diagonal with short legs and every other one with the longer legs.

Sixth, saw to the depth of the gauge lines on the spiral lines which are to be cut. The kerfs will not come out even on the corners but that can be taken care of later.

Seventh, with a sharp chisel cut with the grain toward the saw kerf, until a V-shaped groove takes the place of the diagonal. With a 2-inch leg, the distance across the top of the V will be about 1 inch, and with larger legs the distance will be greater. Do not make this distance too great or the ridges will become too sharp. As soon as this process is completed, bevel each corner to the gauge lines. With a skew chisel or carving knife cut across the corners so that the groove will be continuous.

Finally, with a broad, sharp chisel begin to shape the rope into a continuous spiral. No amount of instruction will help in this process; the only safe procedure is for the worker to go slowly and to be sure he has the grain with him.

The illustration of the leg in the different stages of development will perhaps convey the idea better than any amount of instructions.

The old Spanish colonial spirals were made to appear semisquare. If, however, it is desired to have the legs round instead of semisquare, it is simply necessary to remove more stock

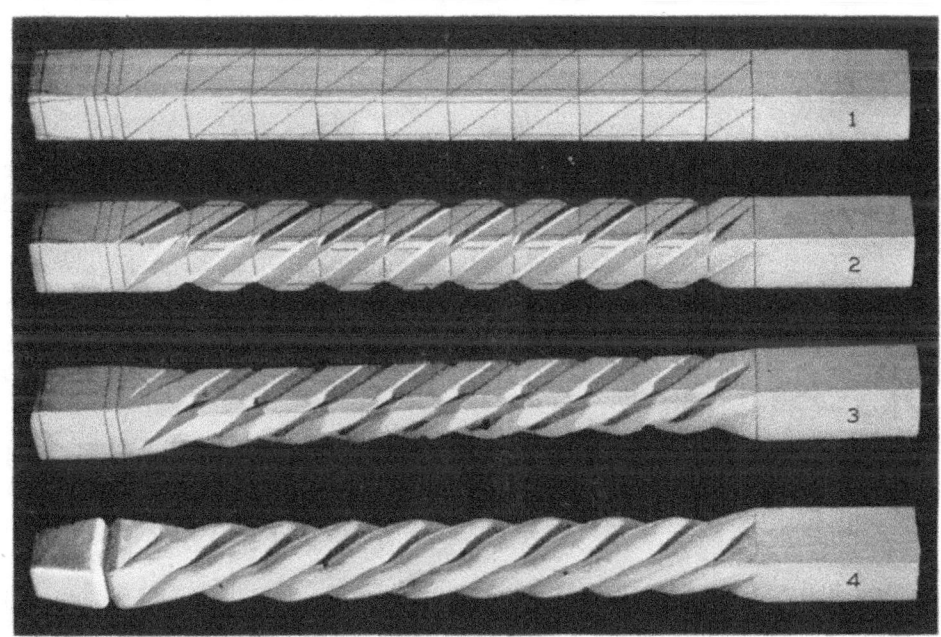

Four steps in carving spiral legs

from the corners until the shape is an octagon. Then the diagonals are run across the eight sides instead of four, and the eight sides are sawed. In this case, it is advisable to leave out every other diagonal in the sawing process so that only four spiral lines run around the piece.

Quite often it is desirable to "rope" a round piece of stock for a table leg, such as a cedar fence post. Cut the piece to the desired length and mark off for rails and feet as in the preceding paragraphs. Smooth the portion to be carved as much as possible, and lay it out in the following manner for carving:

First, take two pieces of string of sufficient length for the spirals, and tie each to a thumbtack opposite each other where the spirals are to begin. Wind one at a time around the piece which is to be carved and fasten it at the other end with a thumbtack. Check the spacing to see that it is carefully equalized, and with a pencil or grease crayon, mark the course of each string.

Second, saw to the desired depth and carve with the grain as directed in the preceding paragraphs.

Knots need not interfere with the carving. Use a heavier chisel and a mallet to cut through them. When carefully smoothed and polished, knots add greatly to the appearance of the furniture.

THE FEET

It is always difficult to work out appropriate and well-proportioned feet for the square-effect spiral leg. With the old Spanish colonial craftsmen, very little attention was given to this element of the design and construction. The chests usually sat directly on the floor. This was also true of the wall cabinets. A fine old chest, repaired in the author's shop, had spherical knobs for feet, fastened by mortise joints to the bottom and wedged. A similarly designed support has been used in the chest shown in this book.

The dimensions for the feet are indicated in the plates, but it is a matter of individual choice as to what type will best suit the work. If a lathe is available, the turned foot looks well with the spiral leg.

CARVED EDGES

The early colonial furniture makers used a variety of carved designs to relieve the plain edges of table tops, the edges of benches, and the tops of chests and wall cabinets. The designs were relatively simple and required very moderate skill in the use of a knife and a skew chisel. Simple chip carving was involved in some of the most widely used designs. The so-called bullet design and the meander are characteristic of the earlier pieces.

It is well for the present-day student of the Spanish colonial furniture to master a variety of the typical edge carving designs. Geometric designs with chip carving have been especially attractive to the author's students. Some of the designs shown in the illustration on page 13 and in the several plates later in the book are easier to make than chip carving designs. A bit of practice with a piece or two of scrap wood will give the workman an idea of the effectiveness of a desired design and will show him what his own skills will make possible. The layouts of the illustrated designs are planned for $1\frac{1}{8}$-inch stock.

DESIGN 1. Run pencil lines $\frac{1}{8}$ inch from each edge for the portion not carved. With the rule, mark off each inch and run vertical lines. Set the T bevel and run diagonals on every other rectangle. Reverse the bevel and run diagonals in the remaining rectangles. With a sharp carving knife or skew chisel, cut the triangles out as depressions, leaving all lines as sharp ridges.

DESIGN 2. Run pencil lines 3/16 inch from both edges. Locate the center of the table or chest top edge, and lay off distances of 4 inches each way from the center. With a sharp, hollow punch cut out a 5/16-inch hole about 3/16 inch deep at the 4-inch intervals. Carve the arcs on each side with a $\frac{3}{4}$-inch gouge about $\frac{1}{8}$ inch deep. Use the same gouge on the rest of the unit. The depressions are from 3/16 inch to $\frac{1}{4}$ inch deep. The design should not be cut too deeply.

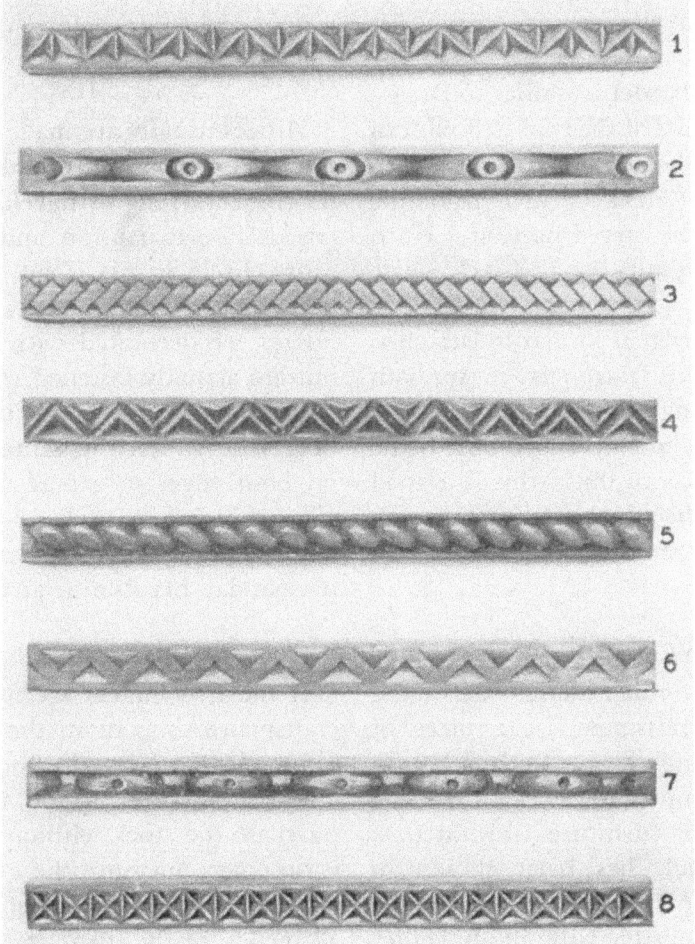

Chip-carving designs

DESIGN 3. Locate the center of each edge to be carved. Run pencil lines 1/8 inch from each of the edges. With the T bevel set at 45 degrees, run diagonal lines 7/16 inch apart the entire length of the edge. Reverse the T bevel and run the triangles from the intersections of these lines. Carve the triangles with a series of chips and run the diagonal lines to a depth of 1/16 inch. For a narrow edge, run the diagonals closer together or use less than a 45-degree angle.

DESIGN 4. Run pencil lines 1/8 inch from the edges. Set the T bevel at 45 degrees. Slide the thumbscrew as near the center of the blade as possible, leaving the slotted part of the blade for running the design. Run a pencil line on each side of the narrow portion of the blade. Reverse and run the two lines.

By this process double lines are run the entire length as in Design 6. Chip out the triangles as in Design 6. Run a third line halfway between them. This third line becomes the center of the meandering V-shaped groove running the entire length of the edge.

DESIGN 5. This is a roped design that looks well on a thick table top. It is a series of parallelograms rounded into the desired effect. Use pencil lines 1/8 inch from the edges, and with a T bevel set at about 35 or 40 degrees, run a series of parallelograms. No amount of instruction will help the worker to complete this design satisfactorily. The best procedure is to take a piece of scrap wood and practice until the desired results are obtained.

DESIGN 6. Lay out this design the same

13

as Design 4. Do the same carving, but do not run the groove in the center of the flat meander surface.

Design 7. This border is similar to Design 2 except that the units of the repeated pattern are smaller. Make the centers 3 inches apart, and run the pencil lines 1/4 inch from the edges. This leaves the carved portion 5/8 inch wide. For the best results use a 1/2-inch gouge to round the units.

Design 8. This edge is similar to Design 1. It is laid out the same. Diagonals are run both ways of the rectangles, making twice the number of triangles to be chipped out. If the top is 1 1/2 inch or more thick, this is a good design to use. For the 1-inch tops, the carving is too intricate for the beginner to do with success.

DRAWER PULLS

The drawer pull most widely made by the Spanish colonial craftsmen was a piece of leather drawn through a hole and nailed on the inside of the drawer.

For the pieces of furniture illustrated, a type of drawer pull has been chosen to resemble the original wooden pulls on old pieces as nearly as possible without altogether losing the ornamental values. A drop pull similar to these pulls was used by the craftsmen of the original thirteen American colonies.

The size of the pull varies with the size of the drawer. The usual size for the chest of drawers or the wall cabinets is a piece 1 1/8 by 1 1/8 by 3 1/2 inches. Bore a hole with a 5/16-inch bit 1 inch deep. Then, with a marking gauge set at 1/4 inch lay off lines on each end from the four sides. Run a line around the piece 5/8 inch from the end without a hole, and from this bevel down to the lines on the two ends. Cut a piece of thick harness leather to fit the hole and nail it into place from the underside with 3/4-inch brads. Use the same bit to bore holes in the drawers, run the leather through, and, allowing enough slack (about 3/4 inch) so the pull will drop into place, nail the leather into place on the inside of the drawer. It is best to cut out a groove on the inside of the drawer for the leather to fit into before nailing.

HINGES

Hinges usually are made to extend entirely across the top of a drop-lid chest to keep the lid from warping or developing a wide open crack. The expansion and contraction may cause checks in the wood, but these seem to be considered desirable features. The typical hinges are decorated with large rivet heads, but are actually fastened with small rivets or screws. The old chests usually had three hinges, of which the center one was hinged on both edges to act as a hasp. The chests were supplied with hand-forged locks with huge keys. These locks can be made by a present-day blacksmith at a cost of $6 to $8.

TWISTED IRON BRACES

If the iron braces are made in the home-craftsman's shop or in the school shop, it is sometimes necessary to find the exact length and size of iron to be used in order to purchase the stock without waste. When this is necessary, measure the exact distance from the center to the stretchers, and add to this 18 inches for the turns at each end, or a total of 36 inches. The exact size and shape of the finished brace is laid out with chalk on the cement floor of the workroom or shop. The iron is twisted while hot and worked into the desired shape. When using a smaller size iron on a small table, allow the same amount for the end spirals as on the large one.

FINISHING THE PIECES

The furniture illustrated in this book is best finished with a wax finish similar to that used by the early Spanish settlers of the Southwest. Beeswax was prepared by them when turpentine was available, to produce a fairly good wax for polishing furniture. At other times sheep tallow was used for that purpose. The tallow was melted and brushed on the wood while hot. This would fill the pores of the wood, preserve it, and keep the moisture out so that it would not warp. As the wood aged, it would turn to a soft brown color, and would take a polish by rubbing with a cloth.

Numerous oxidizing agents can be used to give the pine wood an antique appearance. A solution of potassium dichromate crystals and water has been found very satisfactory. The strength of the solution can be varied to get any shade desired. If about three ounces of crystals to one gallon of water are used, the solution will oxidize the wood and leave it with a greenish tinge when dry. A stronger solution will produce a darker color. It is best to try the stain on a sample of wood until the desired shade is determined. Exposure to the direct rays of the sun while the wood is still wet will also give a darker finish. It is advisable, therefore, that the samples be kept away from the bright sunlight until quite dry. It takes several days before the true color becomes fixed. When pieces of furniture are to be matched for color, the samples should be retained two days before the final staining.

The solution is applied freely to the finished piece of furniture with a brush. When dry, it is sanded lightly with No. 2/0 used sandpaper. It is advisable not to use the sandpaper on a block of wood, but to fold it and use it lightly by pressure with the finger tips. It takes very little sanding to smooth the surface where the grain has been raised by the water solution.

The piece should stand for a few days to be sure that the color is the one desired. If it is too light, another coat of the solution must be applied. It should be kept in mind that Spanish colonial furniture was light in color; it was the natural color of the wood after being exposed to the elements of sunlight and humidity. This light color harmonizes with adobe walls, bright-colored mantas, and Navajo rugs.

When the sanding has been well done, the surface of the wood will feel smooth to the touch. It is necessary to brush the piece thoroughly to get the dust from the carved surfaces. The liquid wax is applied freely. A hardening wax or a self-polishing wax should not be used when it is at all possible to obtain a true liquid wax. When this has thoroughly dried, a light coat of paste wax is applied and is polished in the usual way. To get the best results, two coats of liquid wax are used about three or four days apart, and the piece is allowed to stand for a day or so before applying the paste wax. This liquid wax fills up the pores of the wood and gives a base for the paste wax. Furniture finished in this way should be waxed every week for a while until a soft velvety finish is obtained.

White shellac is sometimes used as a base for the wax finish. It is usually thinned about half and is rubbed down with 2/0 used sandpaper before the wax is used. Preliminary shellacking saves some labor, but it does not bring out the grain of the wood as a true wax finish does. The shellac also retards the oxidizing action of the stain chemicals. When shellac is used on the top of a table to give it a better wearing surface, the same finish should be used on the remaining surfaces as well. If used on the top only, a reddish tinge will develop on this surface after a year or so, while the rest of the piece will continue to have the characteristic greenish tinge.

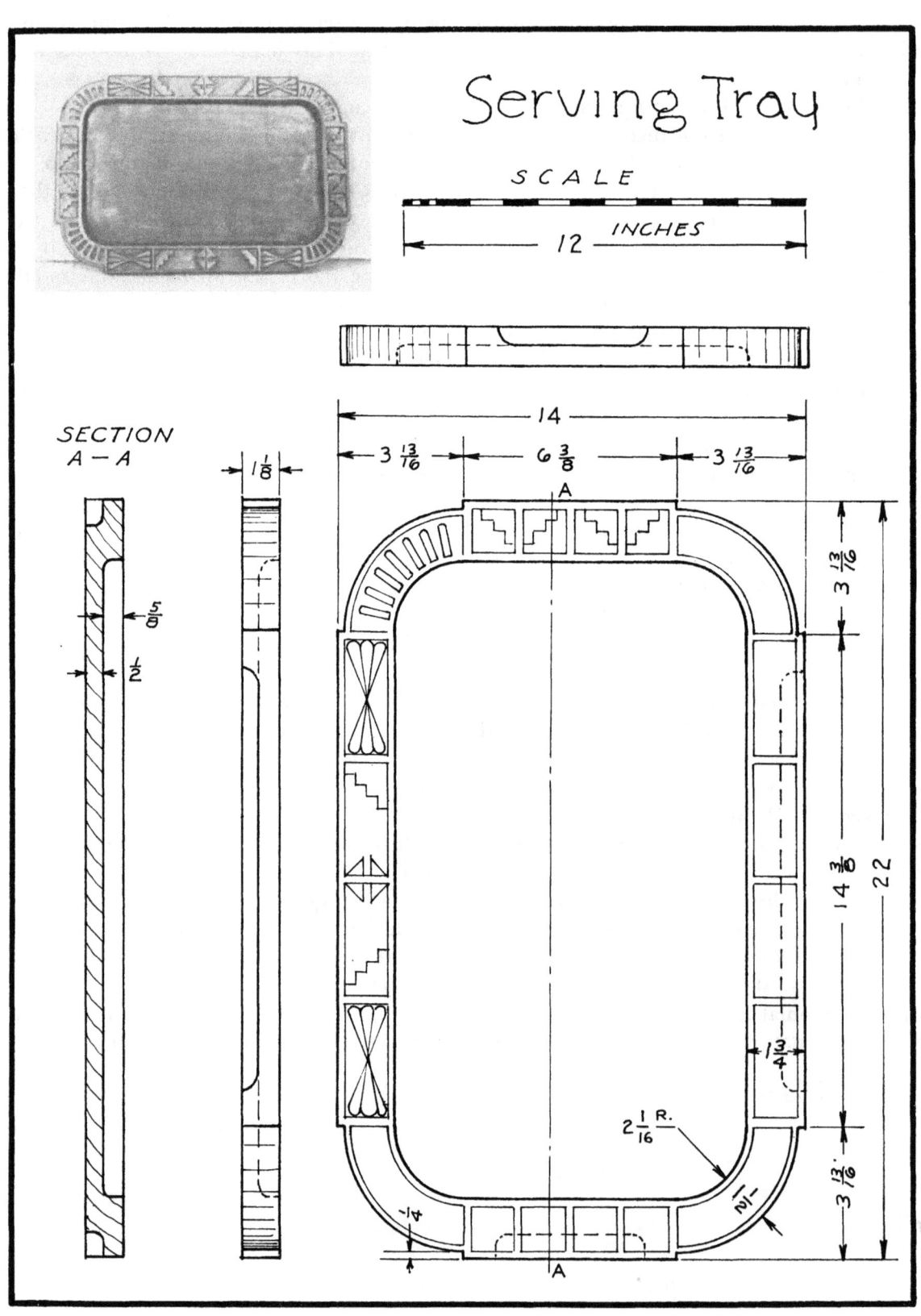

Serving Tray

These trays have been produced with a wide variety of designs. Most of the ornaments are combinations of Indian symbols and, like the Navajo rugs, they depict the soul of the workman. The carver dreams his way through the process of developing a design.

CONSTRUCTION

The tray illustrated is constructed from a piece of white pine 1 1/8 by 14 by 22 inches. The best results are had when the piece of pine is free of sap and is cut from near the center of the tree so it will not warp.

The ends are squared up and the corners are cut. The straight parts of the sides should not be over 1 3/4 inches wide, with the curved parts 1 1/2 inches wide. A wide gouge is used to take out the center to a depth of 5/8 inch, cutting across the grain for the most part. A 2-inch chisel and block plane are used to smooth the bottom. The bottom is often left showing chisel marks.

CARVING

It is next to impossible to give the details of the carving. It is suggested that the workman divide up the space into sections and lay out the design in pencil before starting to carve. Shade in the portion that is to be carved and, with a chisel or gouge, take it out to a depth of about 3/16 inch.

Philippine mahogany, or figured gum, is perhaps more desirable to work with for this project, but very fine results will be had with pine if the tools are kept sharp. Tools always should be kept in good condition.

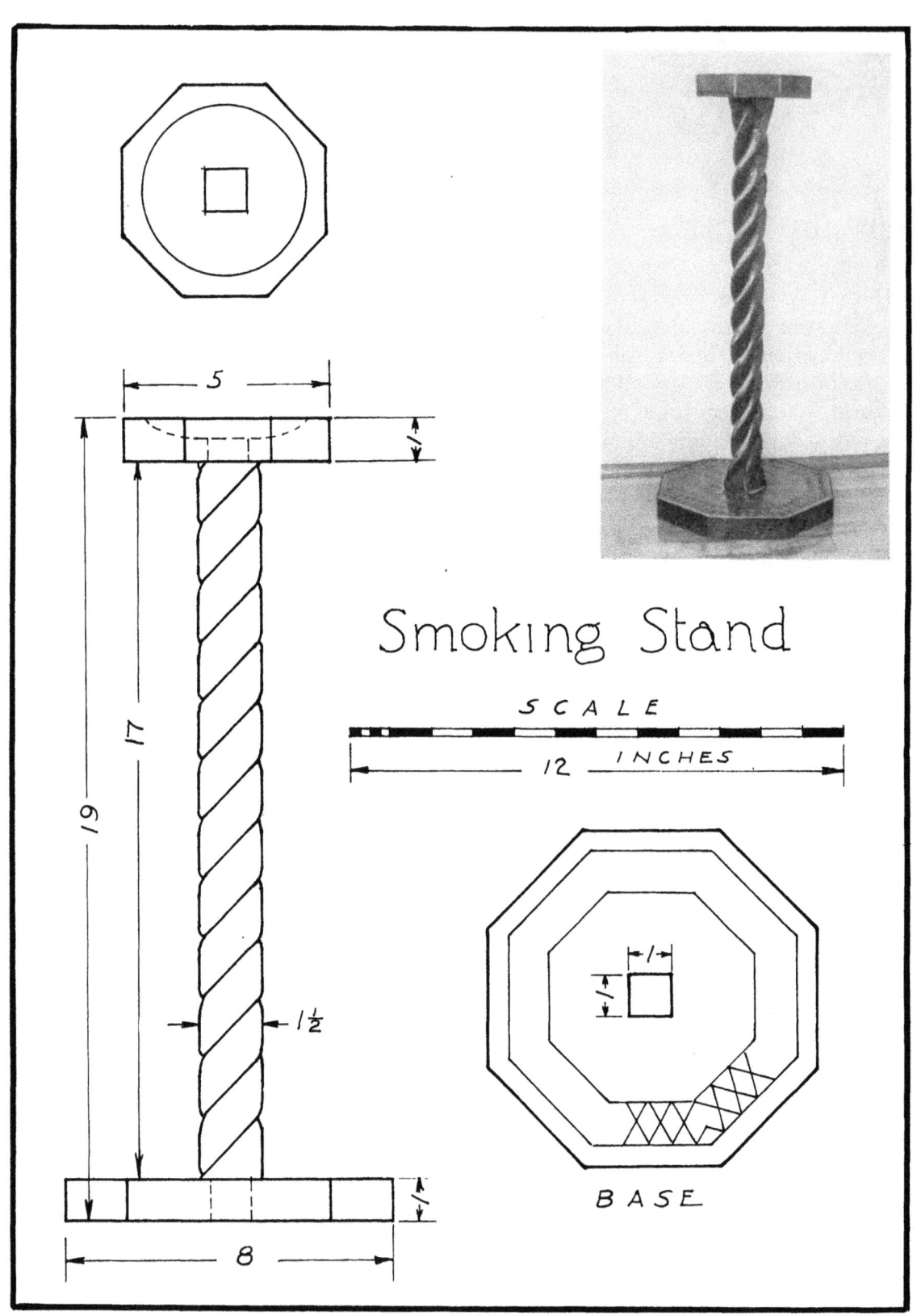

Smoking Stand

SCALE 12 INCHES

BASE

Smoking Stand

BILL OF MATERIAL

Pieces

1	1½ by 1½ by 18½	Stand
1	1 by 8 by 8	Base
1	1 by 5 by 5	Top

The smoking stand is designed in keeping with the Spanish mode. The roping, which is not difficult, offers a good exercise in carving for the beginner.

CONSTRUCTION

The upright is cut from 2-inch stock. The tenons are cut on each end before the piece is laid out for carving. The spirals are run close together, one progressing from each corner of the upright.

The top and bottom pieces are laid out with the help of a compass or 45-degree angle. A circle is inscribed in the square, and the circumference is divided into eight equal parts by bisecting each quadrant of the circle. The tenons should reach nearly through the top and entirely through the bottom. The top may be hollowed out for a metal ash tray by the use of a ½-inch gouge.

CARVING

The spiral carving can be deep or shallow as desired. The deep carving will look better. The design on the base is optional. Some carving should be done to break up the large flat base surface.

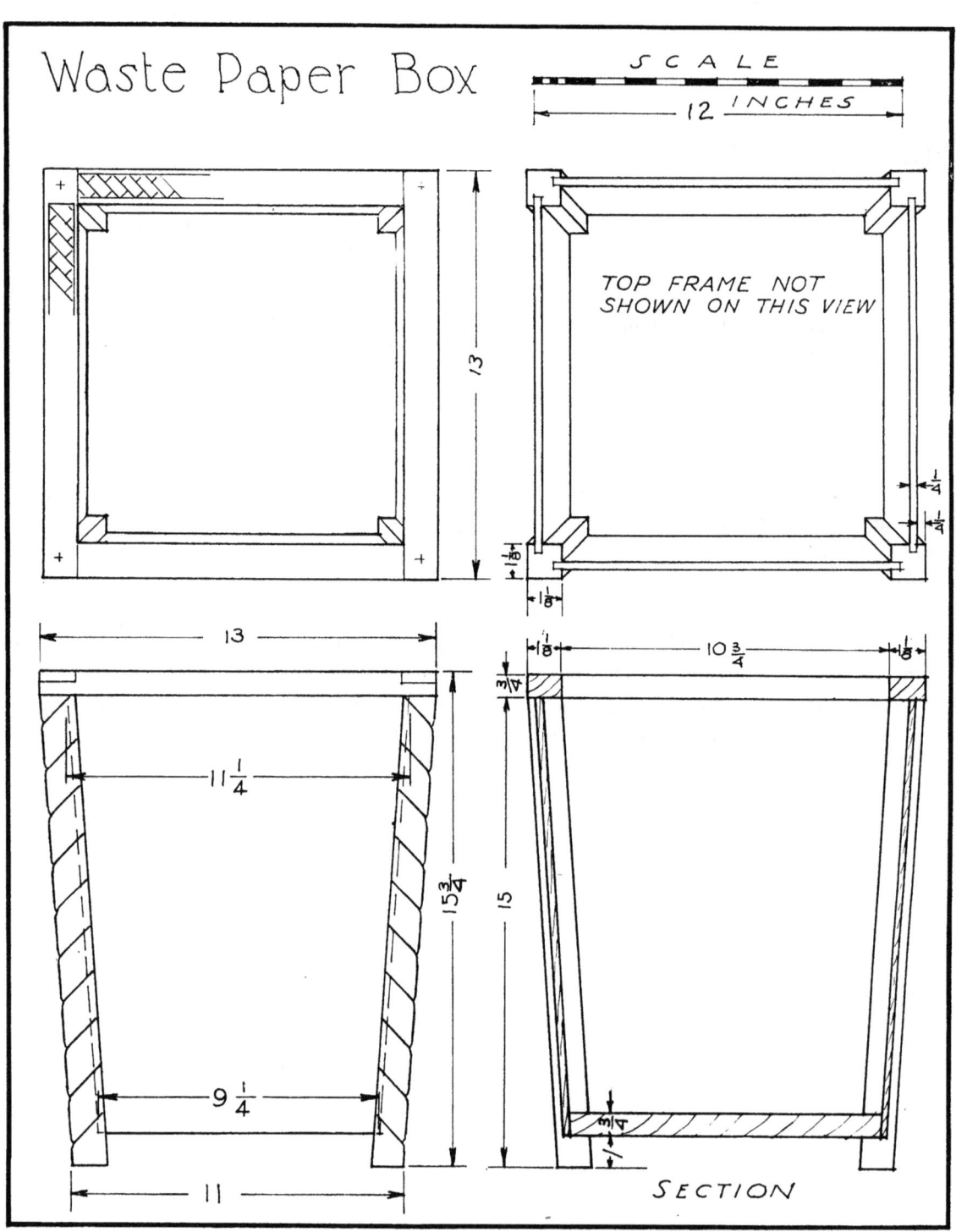

Wastepaper Box

BILL OF MATERIAL

Pieces

4	1⅛ by 1⅛ by 15	Legs
4	¼ by 11¼ by 14	Sides
4	¾ by 1⅛ by 13	Top frame
1	¾ by 10¼ by 10¼	Bottom

A wastepaper basket or box is a practical necessity in the living room and home library. During Spanish colonial times it probably was unknown. This box is relatively a modern invention.

CONSTRUCTION

The four legs are cut to length. Two grooves are cut in each leg with the ¼-inch dado head about ¼ inch from the outside of the leg. The four sides are cut from ¼-inch plywood. They are 1 inch shorter at the bottom than at the top. The sides and legs are glued together, tied up with heavy twine, and set aside overnight for the glue to set.

The frame is made for the top, using a half-lap joint on the corners. This is glued up and clamped. The bottom is of ¾-inch material. It is cut to fit and notched for the corners. It is fastened in place by nailing from each corner. The sides are nailed to the bottom with brads. The top frame is fastened on with 2-inch, No. 10 roundhead screws.

CARVING

After the legs are grooved, the spiral carving is done on the two outer sides. The top frame is laid out into a number of adjacent parallelograms. The triangles are chipped out, and the lines between are run about 1/16 inch deep. The corners are left smooth.

Hall Tree

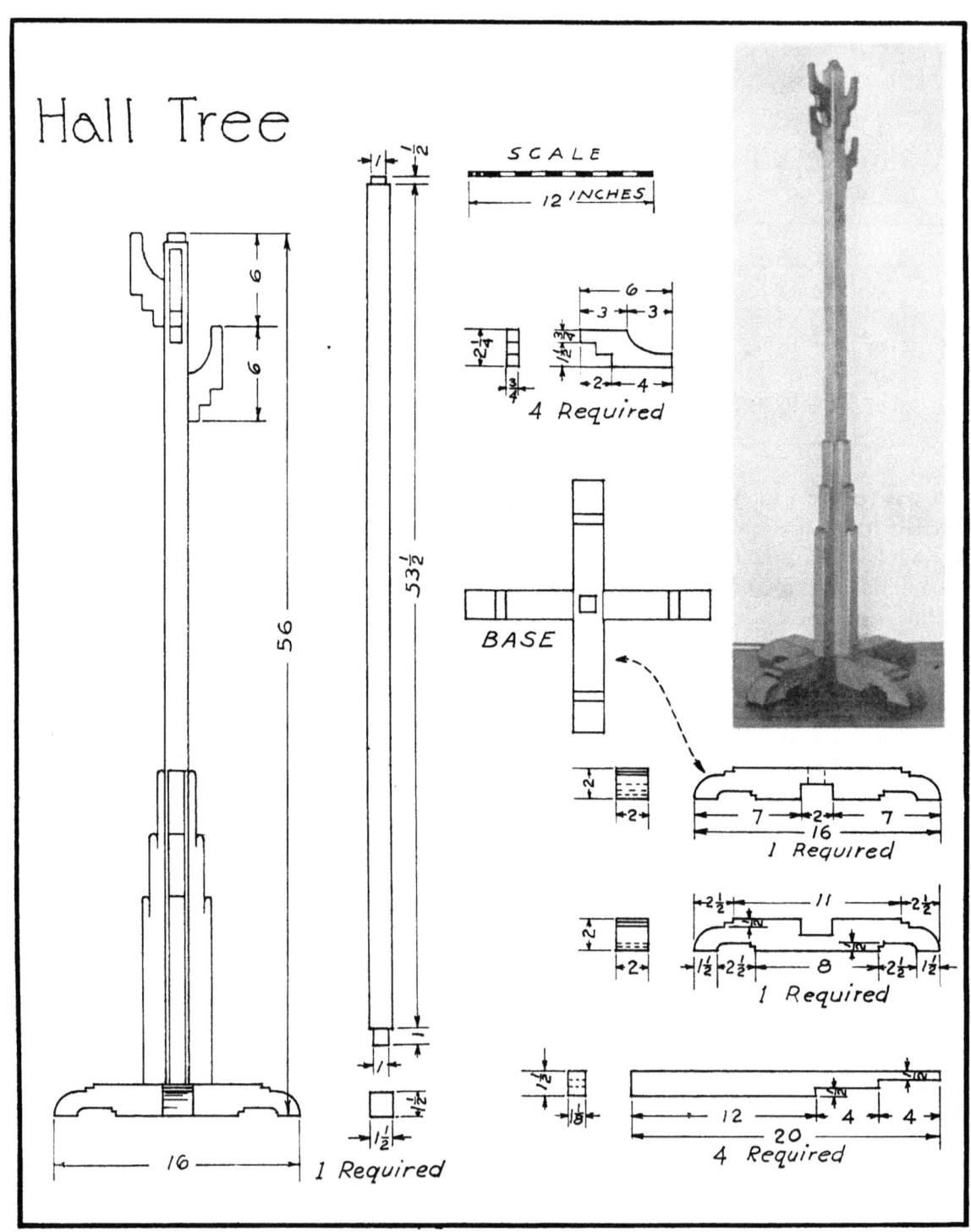

Hall Tree

BILL OF MATERIAL

Pieces		
1	1½ by 1½ by 55	Upright
2	2 by 2 by 16	Base
4	1⅛ by 1½ by 20	Braces
4	¾ by 2¼ by 6	Hooks

The hallway of the modern home must give a favorable impression. It should tell the stranger and the occasional visitor about those who live within. It should suggest an atmosphere of quiet and comfort. A carved drop-lid chest and a hall tree will assist in making the proper introductions.

CONSTRUCTION

A hall tree should be properly proportioned, so the dimensions given in the drawing should be followed rather closely. However, the base can be made slightly heavier than shown. The two base pieces are cut the same size and shape. They are joined with a half-lap joint and glued together. The tenon on the lower end of the standard should be made as heavy as possible and should be at least 1 inch long. The braces for the sides are glued and nailed into place. The hooks should be made of oak or some hardwood that will not split. Each hook is fastened in place with two screws.

CARVING

There is no carving, except for the rounding of the tops of the braces and the hooks. Some simple design could be used on the upright.

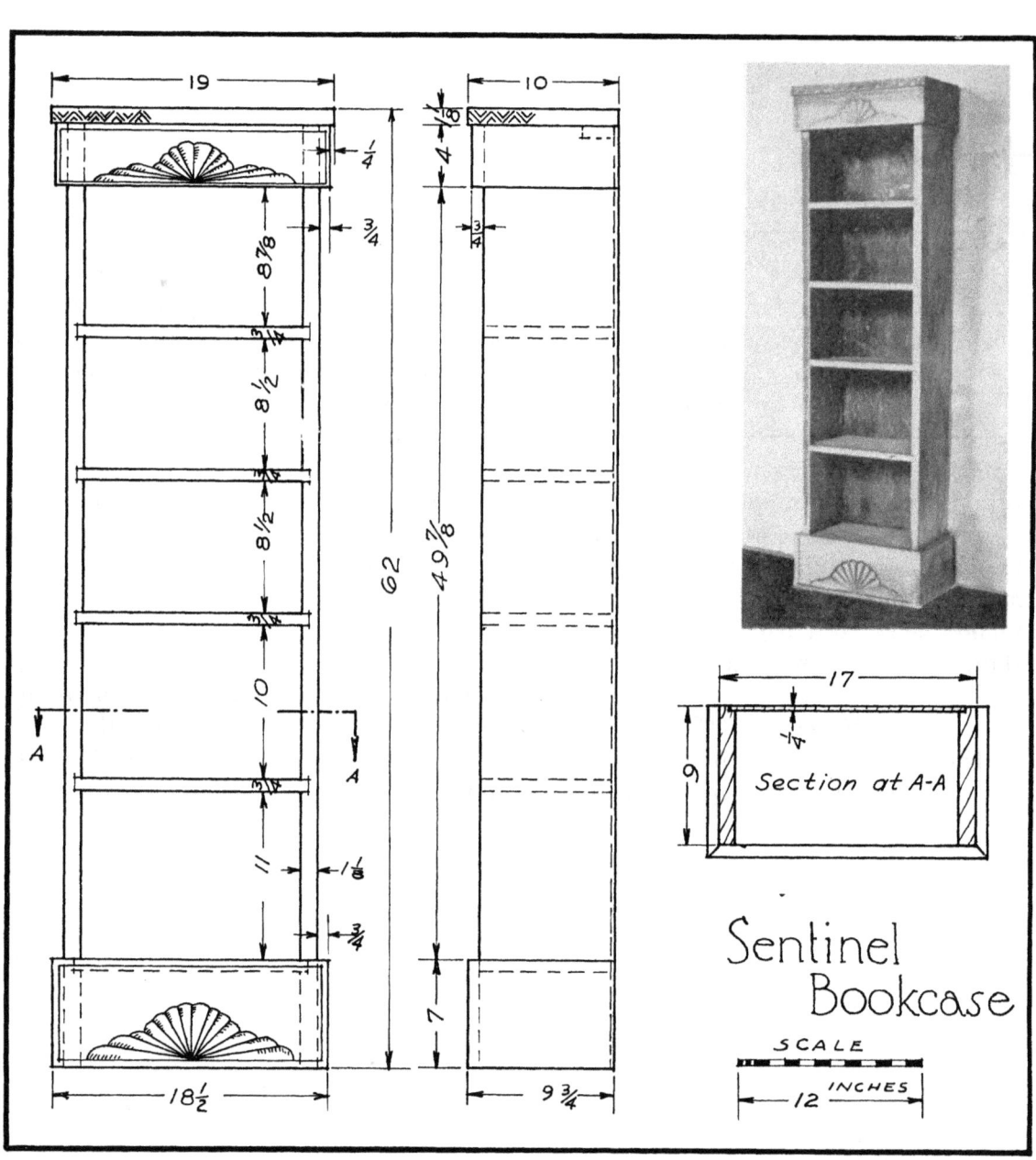

Sentinel Bookcase

BILL OF MATERIAL

Pieces		
2	1⅛ by 9 by 60⅞	Ends
5	¾ by 8¾ by 15¾	Shelves
1	1⅛ by 10 by 19	Top
2	¾ by 4 by 9¾	Facing at top
1	¾ by 4 by 18½	Facing at top
2	¾ by 7 by 9¾	Facing at bottom
1	¾ by 7 by 18½	Facing at bottom
1	¼ by 15¼ by 60⅞	Back
1	¾ by 2½ by 14¾	Top support

A well-designed and carefully executed bookcase of this type is distinctive and decidedly useful. It can be used to advantage in a small room where the wall space is limited, and it is not out of place in a large living room. A pair of Sentinel cases, one on each side of a tall fireplace, add spaciousness to a room. In addition to books, a case of this kind can be used for displaying art objects, particularly pottery, knickknacks, and other small articles of beauty and utility.

CONSTRUCTION

The construction is very simple. The ends are cut to the full height indicated in the plate. They are grooved for the shelves and the back, and are then glued up. The shelves are made ¼ inch narrower than the ends to allow for the back panel. During construction the case must be carefully tested for squareness. In order to avoid nail holes in the facing, a ¾-inch piece can be notched into the top and bottom. The facing can then be secured by the use of glue, and fastened with screws from the inside.

CARVING AND DESIGN

The feather design and the half rosette are thrown in relief by cutting away the background to a depth of about ⅛ inch. In this instance the background is left smooth and sanded to be in keeping with the facing across the ends. The end design is made by drawing two concentric circles with a difference of 9/16 inch in radius. The space between the circles is divided into 24 units, and is chipped out by alternate grooves and ridges. Alternate surfaces of this design are painted dull blue and red, which adds to the beauty of the piece. In Spanish colonial times this design was used quite extensively for decorative purposes.

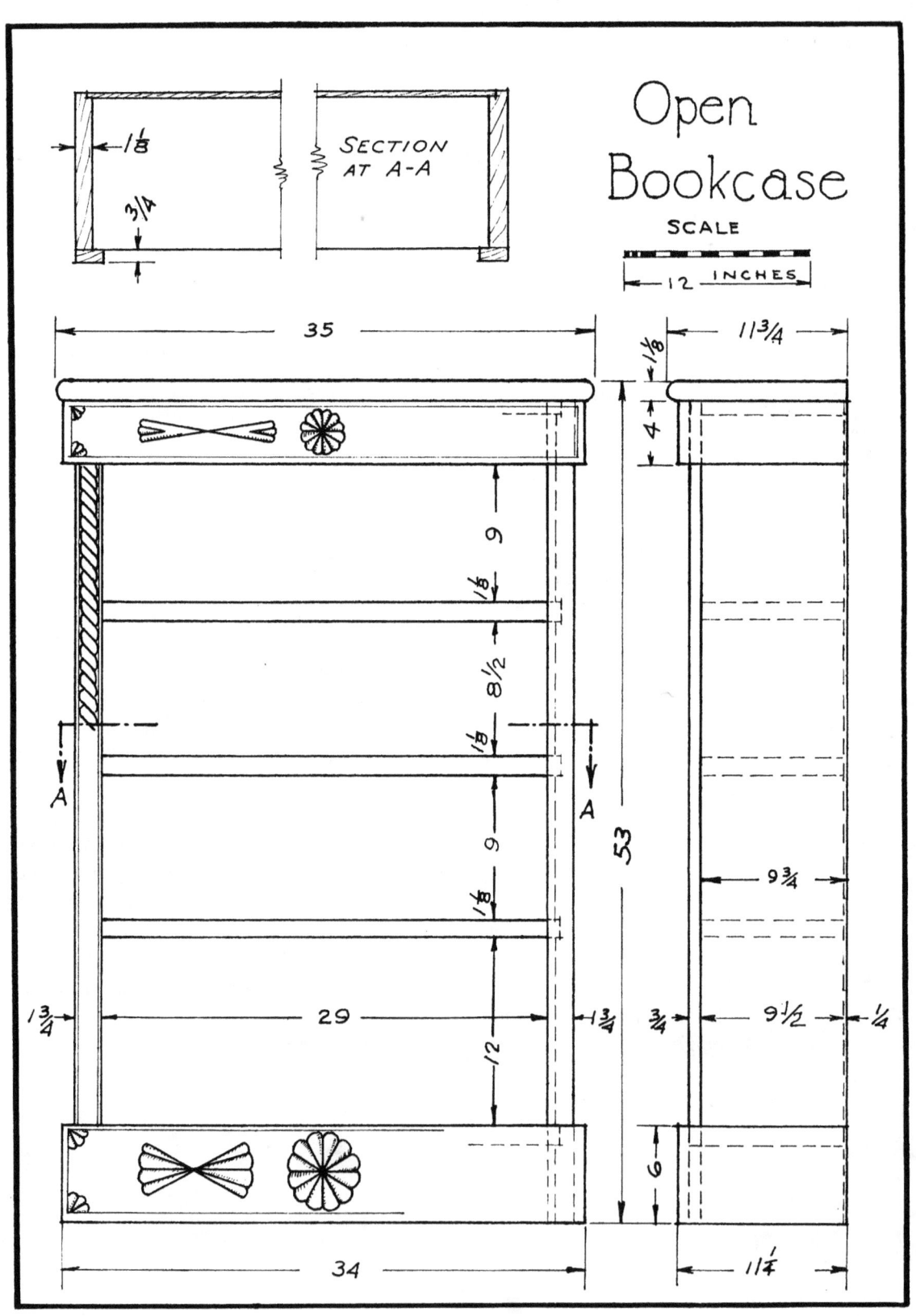

Open Bookcase

BILL OF MATERIAL
Pieces

2	1⅛ by 9¾ by 51⅞	Sides
3	1⅛ by 9½ by 31¼	Shelves
1	1⅛ by 10¼ by 31¼	Bottom shelf
1	¾ by 9½ by 31¼	Piece under top
1	¾ by 6 by 34	Base front
2	¾ by 6 by 11¼	Base sides
1	¾ by 4 by 34	Front apron
2	¾ by 4 by 11¼	Side aprons
1	1⅛ by 11¾ by 35	Top
2	¾ by 1¾ by 51⅞	Facing
1	¼ by 31¼ by 51⅞	Back

The present-day Spanish colonial-type home must have bookshelves or a bookcase where a number of select volumes can be kept for ready reference. Two of these bookcases could be used in a living room, one on each side of the fireplace. The cases may be placed most appropriately in a study or a den. A bookcase is one of the necessary items in the furnishing of a present-day home.

CONSTRUCTION

The sides of 1⅛-inch stock are cut to the desired length. They are grooved ⅝ inch deep to take the shelves and the crosspiece on top. To this piece the top is secured. The top of the lowest shelf should be 6 inches from the floor. The bottom unit should be glued up and tested for squareness. A piece should be fitted in place below the bottom shelf to fasten the facing, and the same procedure should be followed for the top. This will avoid nail holes showing. If preferred, screws can be used. To allow for the back panel, the shelves are cut ¼ inch narrower than the sides. The shelves can be cut ¾ inch less than the sides and ½ inch may be allowed for the facing. Then it is necessary to use 1⅛-inch facing and notch it so the glue will hold on two sides. This will eliminate the use of nails on the facing. At the top and bottom the facing is mitered on the corners and fastened with screws from the inside or nailed from the outside.

CARVING

Possibly too many carved elements are included in the plate, but that is for the individual to consider. The case looks well, however, and the figures blend well. All outlines should be well rounded to bring out the grain of the wood. The spirals are done by cutting a kerf for the center section about ¼ inch deep and 5/16 inch from the edges. The diagonal lines are run with the T bevel, dividing the center section into parallelograms. The corners of the parallelograms are rounded with a knife or a skew chisel to get the desired effect.

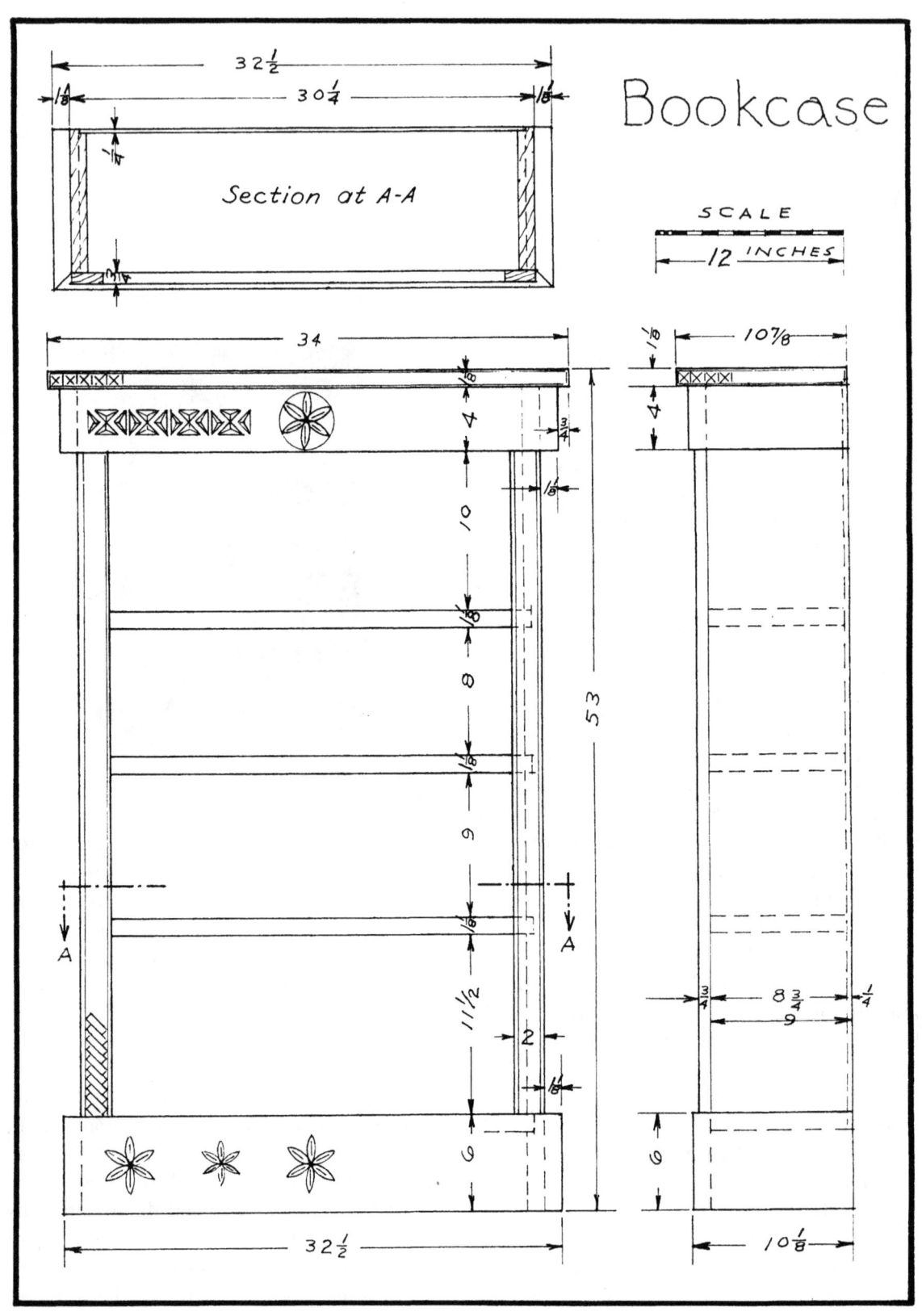

Bookcase

BILL OF MATERIAL

Pieces

2	1⅛ by 9 by 51⅞	Ends
4	1⅛ by 8¾ by 29	Shelves
1	1⅛ by 10⅞ by 34	Top
1	1⅛ by 6 by 32½	Bottom front facing
2	1⅛ by 6 by 10⅛	Bottom end facings
1	1⅛ by 4 by 32½	Top front facing
2	¾ by 4 by 10⅛	Top end facings
2	¾ by 2 by 41⅞	Side end facings
1	¼ by 28½ by 47	Back

An open bookcase is more suitable to the Spanish type of home than a closed one. Shelves similar to these are often used for the display of pottery.

CONSTRUCTION

The sides are cut to the desired length and grooved ½ inch deep to take the shelves and crosspieces on the top. The shelves are glued in place and tested for squareness. A piece is notched in across the top and bottom to fasten the front facing. The facing is secured in place by the use of screws from the inside. The 2-inch facing on the sides is secured with glue and nails, the heads of the nails hidden by the carving. The nailing can be eliminated if the facing is grooved so the glue can hold on two sides.

CARVING

The carved designs are rather simple and easy to do. The spiral carving on the side facing is done by laying out a series of parallelograms and rounding the corners to give the spiral effect. The figures across the top facing are chip carvings with rounded edges in the cuts. The design on the edge of the top is explained in the special chapter on carving.

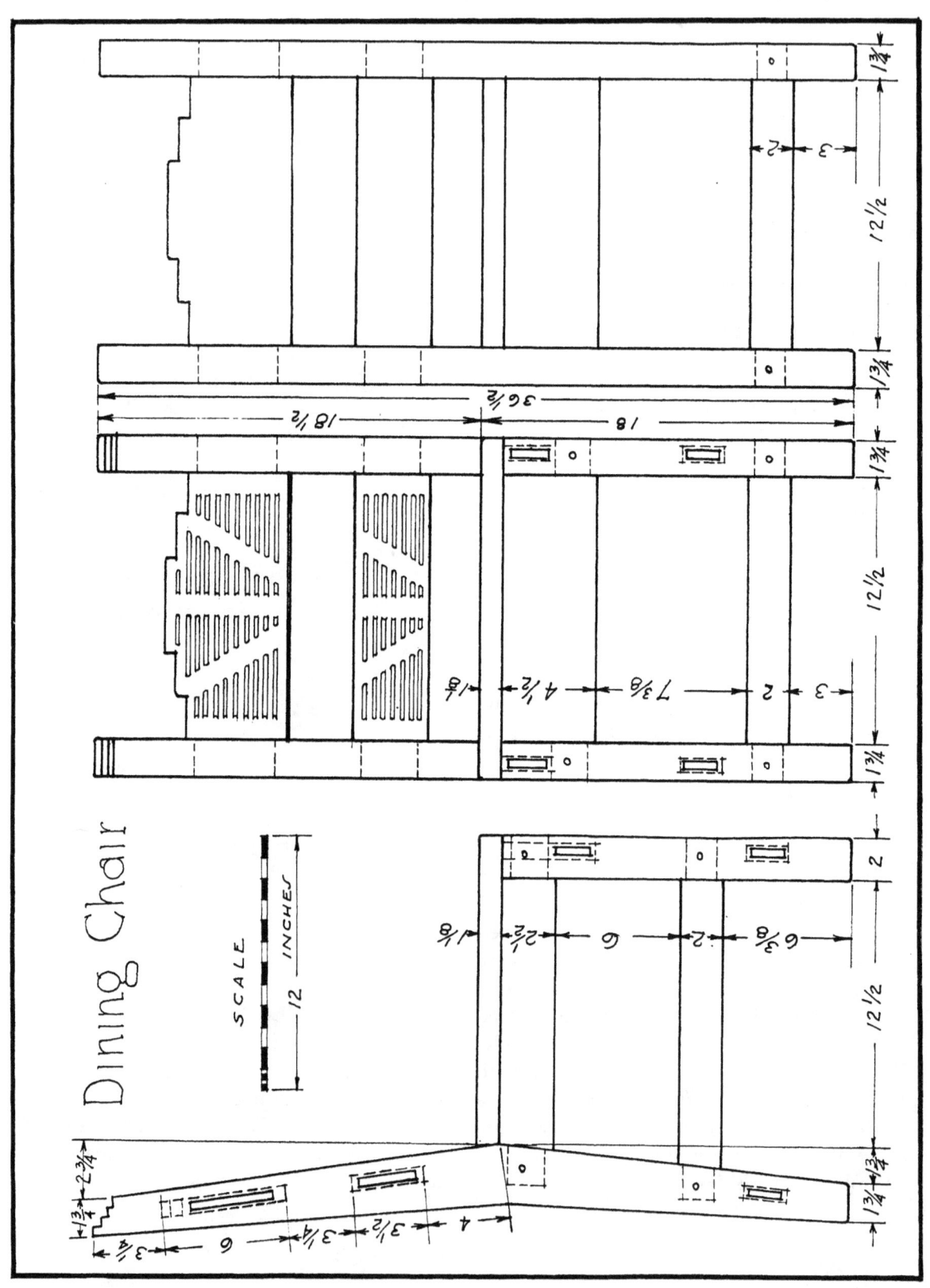

Dining Chair

BILL OF MATERIAL

Pieces
2	1¾ by 4½ by 36½	Back legs
2	1¾ by 2 by 16⅞	Front legs
1	¾ by 6 by 16	Top backpiece
1	¾ by 3½ by 16	Middle backpiece
1	¾ by 2 by 16	Bottom backpiece
1	¾ by 4½ by 16	Frontpiece
2	¾ by 2½ by 16	Top side rails
2	¾ by 2 by 16½	Bottom stretchers
1	1⅛ by 14½ by 16	Seat

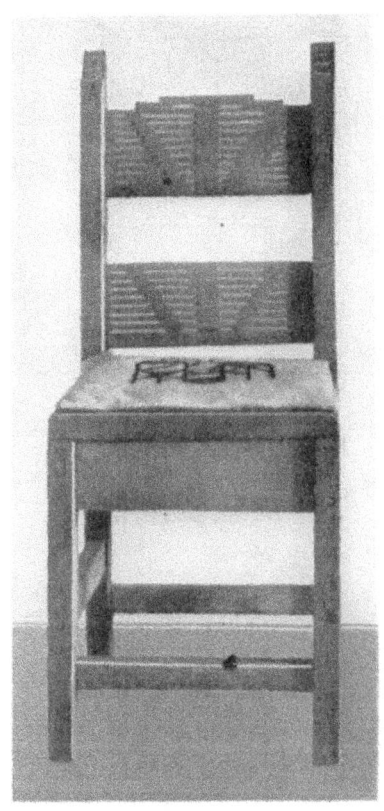

This chair is typical of the dining-room chairs used in the early homes of the Southwest. The carving is not difficult; the structure is conventional. For the backs one could use a great variety of designs that would fit in well with other pieces of furniture.

CONSTRUCTION

The parts are joined by through mortise-and-tenon joints except where the side rails fit into the back legs. Here a blind mortise and tenon is used, the tenon being 1½ inches long and nearly the full width of the rail. The tenon on the front leg is cut away so the side rails can come through the front legs. The back crosspieces are wide to make the chair comfortable. These backpieces must be carved to lighten the appearance of the chair.

CARVING

The offset tops of the back legs blend well with the crosspieces on the back. The backpieces are laid out for carving by drawing horizontal lines. The surface is divided by alternate ⅛- and ¼-inch lines, and the ¼-inch space is carved out with a gouge.

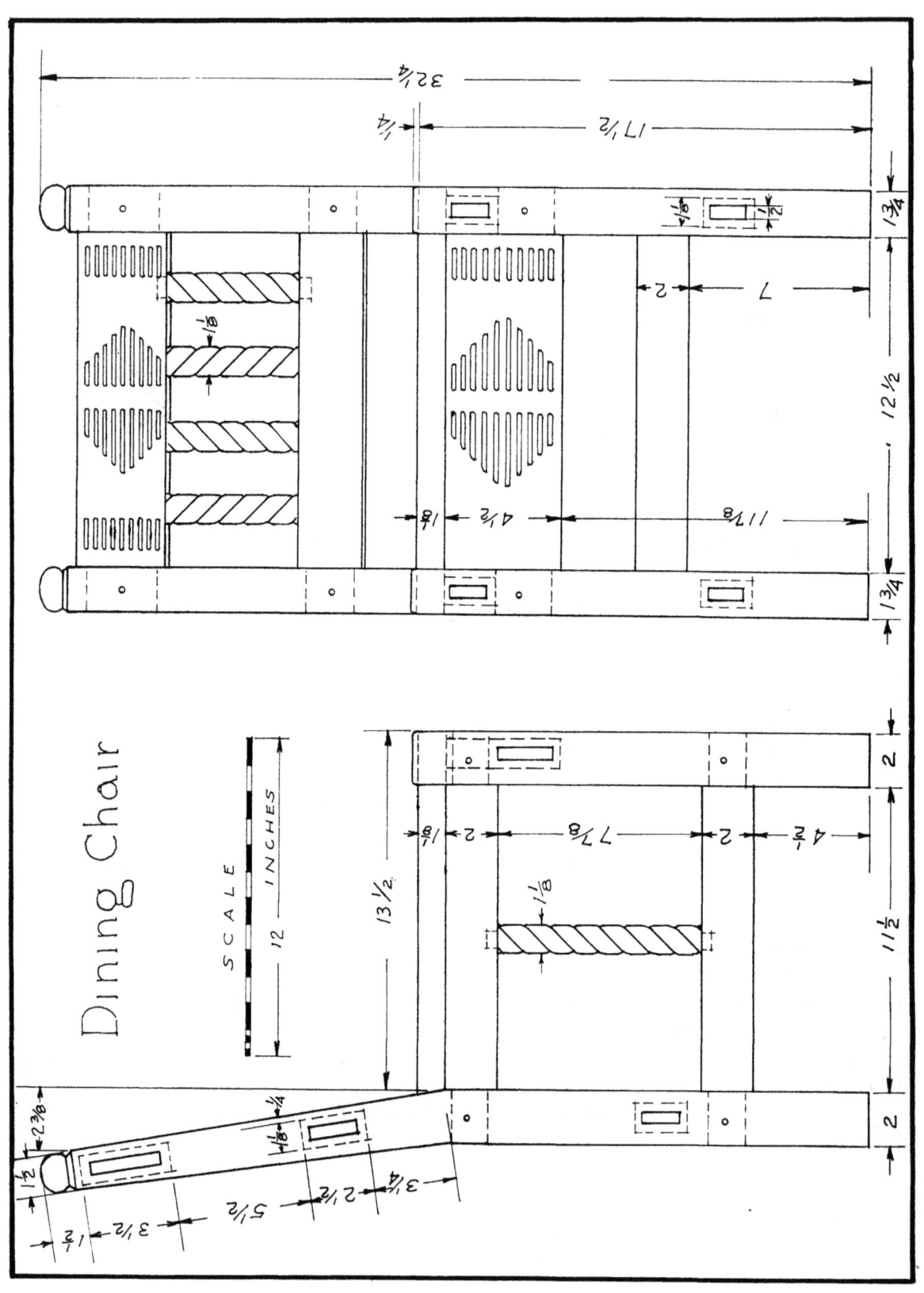

Dining Chair

BILL OF MATERIAL

Pieces

2	1¾ by 2 by 17¾	Front legs
2	1¾ by 3⅞ by 32¼	Back legs
1	1⅛ by 3½ by 16	Back crosspiece
1	1⅛ by 2½ by 16	Back crosspiece
1	1⅛ by 2 by 16	Back crosspiece
1	1⅛ by 4½ by 16	Front crosspiece
4	1⅛ by 2 by 15½	Side pieces
2	1⅛ by 1⅛ by 8⅞	Side spirals
4	1⅛ by 1⅛ by 6½	Back spirals
1	1⅛ by 13¾ by 16	Seat

This chair has features characteristic of the Spanish colonial type without being a direct copy. The spirals are characteristic of Old Spain. They were chosen to harmonize with the dining-room table with spiral legs.

This chair is comfortable and sturdy enough to stand heavy use. It may be used as a beginner's project. It can be roughly made and still hold up, and it has a large variety of operations that make it well adapted to instruction.

CONSTRUCTION

The construction is simple and is indicated in the plate. Through mortise-and-tenon joints are used. They should be glued as well as pinned. Square pins would possibly characterize the early period better, but either kind may be used. All pieces should be cut to fit before the spirals are marked for tenons. It is best to cut the tenons and fit all pieces together before doing any carving.

CARVING

The carving on the crosspieces is done with a ¼-inch carving gouge. The design is laid out first, using ⅜-inch divisions on the rule, ¼ inch to be carved out, and ⅛ inch between. The spirals are close together, a groove traveling from each corner while usually a groove travels from every other corner. The knobs on the top could be longer and higher. They are cut with a chisel and are rounded with a cabinet file.

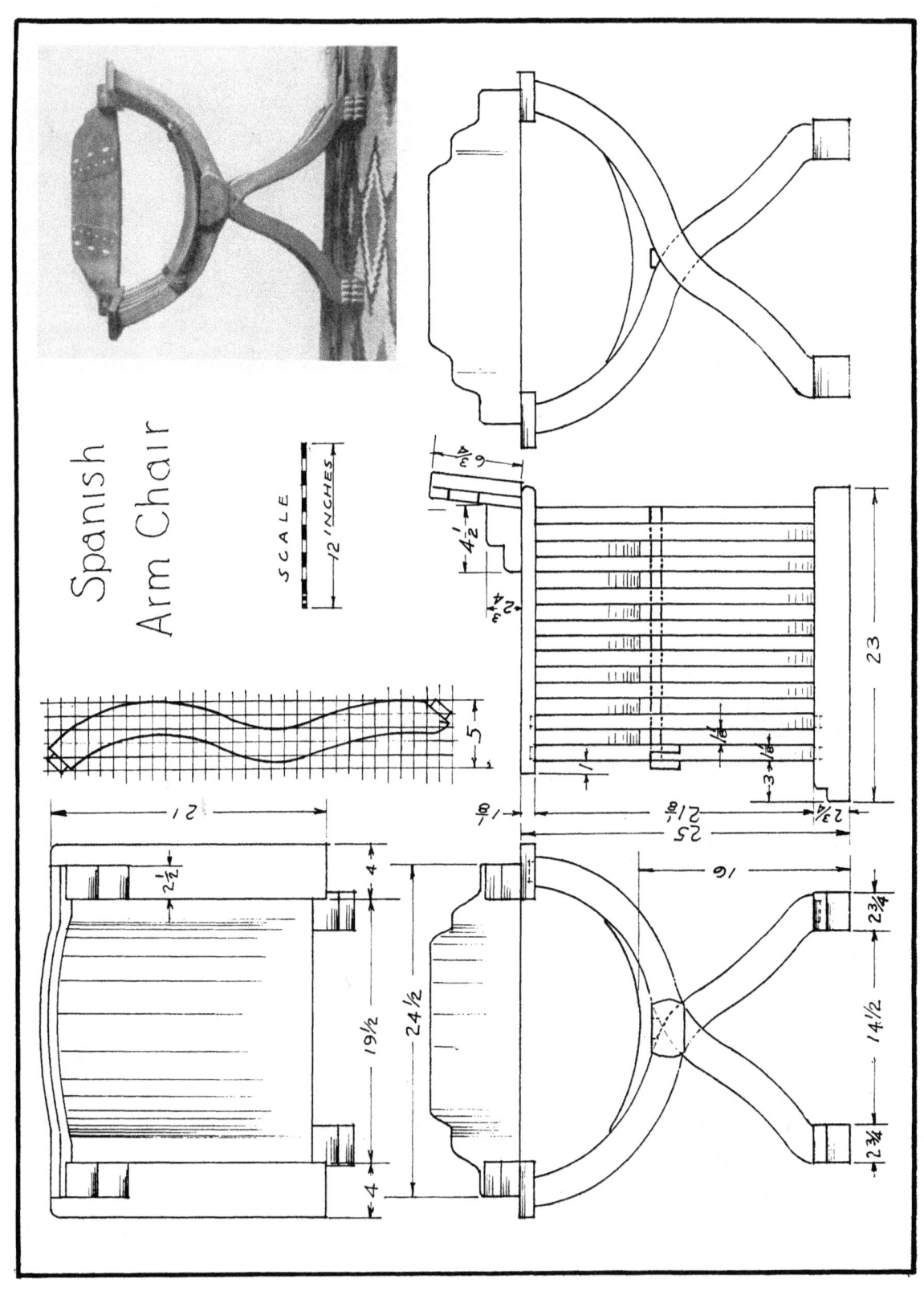

Spanish Armchair

BILL OF MATERIAL

Pieces		
17	1⅛ by 5 by 31	Legs
2	2¾ by 2¾ by 23	Feet
2	1⅛ by 4 by 21	Arms
1	2 by 6¾ by 24½	Back
2	2½ by 2¾ by 4½	Braces
1	leather, 18 by 18	Seat
1	1 by 1½ by 18	Brace under seat
1	½ by 3 by 5	Front decorative piece

While this chair is distinctly Spanish, it can be used in any home. It is attractive and when constructed properly is strong. The main disadvantage is the fact that a considerable amount of material must be wasted in cutting the legs.

CONSTRUCTION

A template is laid out as shown in the plate. A piece of ¼-inch plywood will serve the purpose. Seventeen pieces are cut from 1⅛-inch material. The two frontpieces are joined with a cross-lap joint, so they will be flush; all other pieces alternate and are spaced evenly by a piece under the seat. The two backpieces are fastened with screws but do not half lap. The pieces can be fastened to the arms with screws, or they can be mortised as shown in the plate. Blocks are fastened to the tops of the arms with glue and screws from beneath. The back is secured in position with 3-inch No. 16 screws. It is shaped from a single piece, 2 inches or more in thickness. If a heavy 2-inch piece is not available, stock may be glued up for the purpose, as was done in this chair shown.

DESIGN

No carving is done in the project. If the arms are fastened to the legs with screws, the heads should be covered with inlay. The back is glued-up stock, secured with dowel pins and screws, the heads of which are covered with inlay. Harness leather or rawhide is used for the seat. This leather is secured in place with 3d nails, which in turn are covered with ornamental nails.

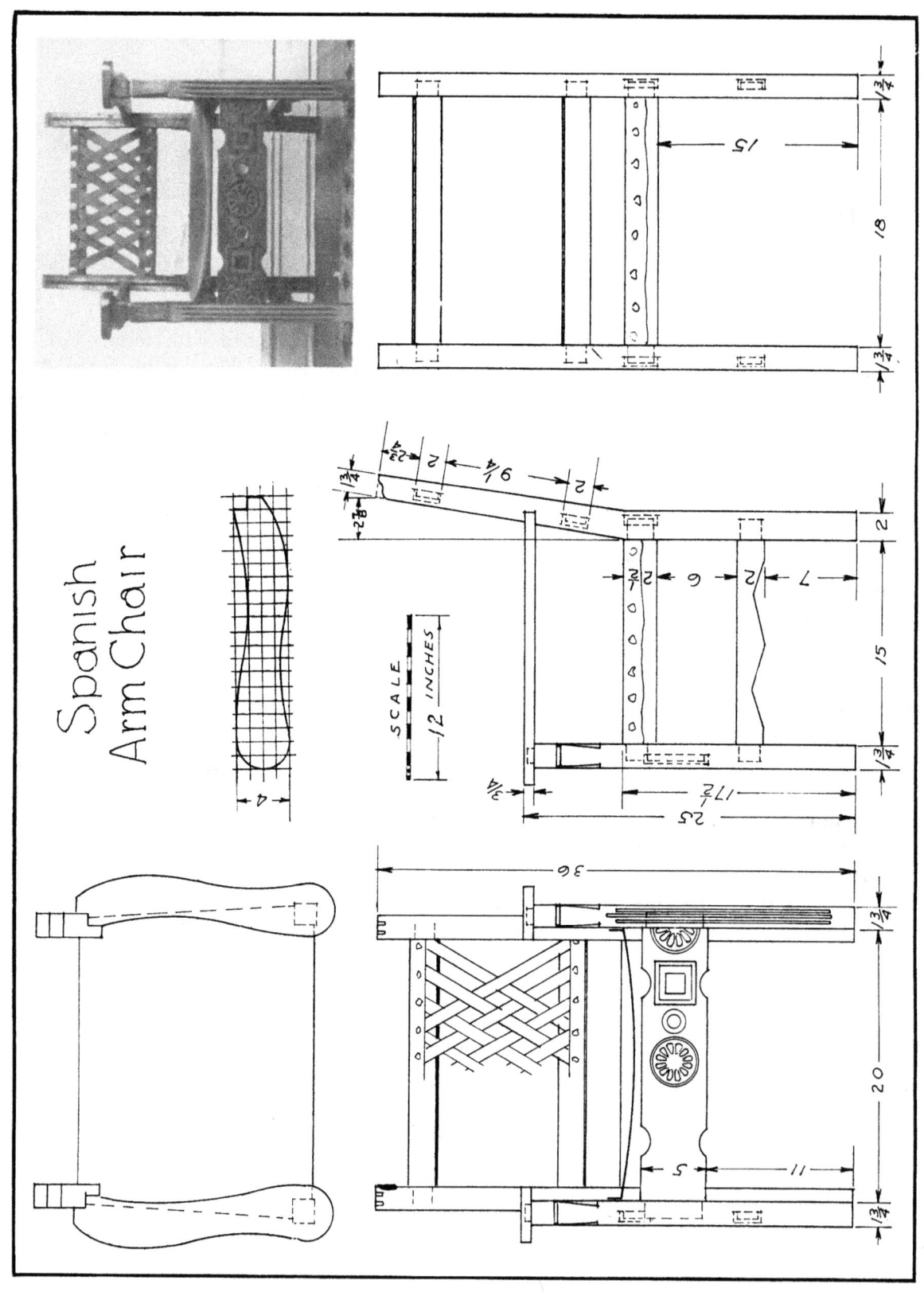

Spanish Arm Chair

Spanish Armchair

BILL OF MATERIAL
Pieces

2	1¾ by 1¾ by 24¾	Front legs
2	1¾ by 4⅝ by 36	Back legs
3	1⅛ by 2 by 20½	Back crosspieces
1	1⅛ by 5 by 22½	Front stretcher
2	1⅛ by 2½ by 17½	Side rails
2	1⅛ by 2 by 17½	Side stretchers
2	¾ by 4 by 20	Arms
4	Dozen ornamental nails	

Leather for seat and back

A chair of this type is both artistic and comfortable. It carries an atmosphere of Old Spain and is well suited to the present home in which Spanish forms are reproduced.

CONSTRUCTION

Blind mortise-and-tenon joints are used in the construction of this chair. The tenons should be as long as possible. On the front stretcher the tenons should be pinned because of the heavy pull of the suspended seat. The shape of the side stretchers, which were copied from an old Spanish piece, is optional.

CARVING

The carving on the front stretcher is easily done. The elements of the rosette are taken out with a gouge. The design is not unusual, and is typically Spanish. The back can be rawhide strips, secured with ornamental nails. The seat is of heavy cowhide leather that does not stretch. The fluting on the front legs is done with a ¼-inch gouge. If desired other devices may be used to lighten the appearance.

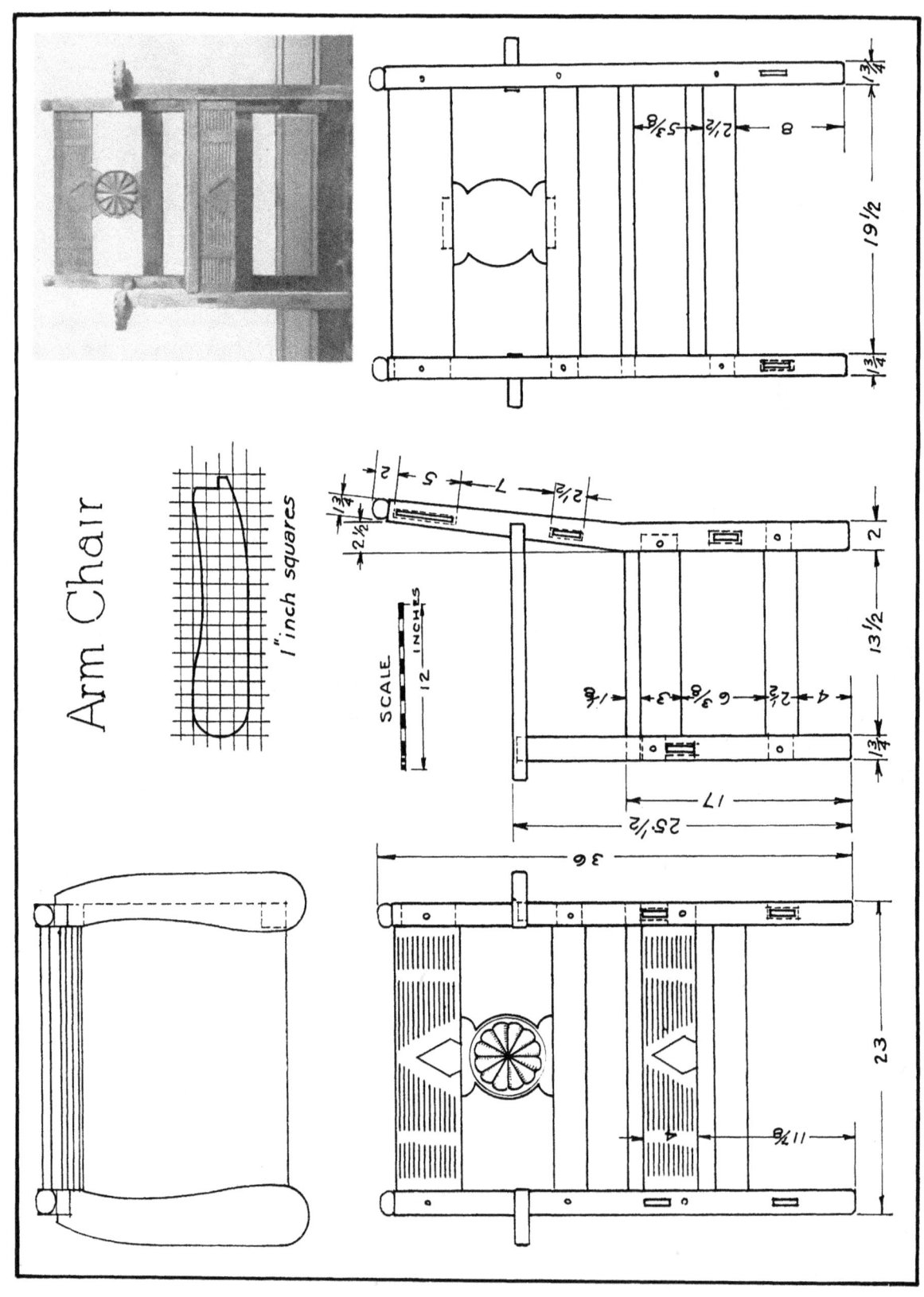

Armchair

BILL OF MATERIAL

Pieces			
2	1¾ by 1¾ by 25⅛	Front legs
2	1¾ by 4¼ by 36	Rear legs
1	1⅛ by 4 by 23	Front apron
1	1⅛ by 5 by 23	Upper back rail
1	¾ by 2½ by 23	Lower back rail
1	1⅛ by 2½ by 23	Rear stretcher
2	1⅛ by 2½ by 17¼	Side stretchers
2	1⅛ by 3 by 16½	Side aprons
1	1⅛ by 15¼ by 23	Seat
2	1⅛ by 4 by 19	Arms
1	¾ by 6½ by 8½	Back

This armchair is much more comfortable than it appears. It is light, easily moved, and is a convenient utility piece. The seat is low so a pillow-type cushion can be used. The pillow, which is not shown here, is made of monk's cloth and is decorated with Pueblo embroidery.

CONSTRUCTION

The construction is similar to that of other chairs described. The back is the same width as the front, so that the beginner in woodwork will have very little difficulty in the joinery. The frontpiece supporting the seat is wide enough so the tenon can be cut on the lower half to miss the tenons coming through from the side rails. No braces are necessary. The seat is fastened to the rails with hidden screws, the heads of which are countersunk and covered with square pins. All joints are glued and pinned.

CARVING AND FINISH

The carving is characteristically Spanish colonial. In the old chairs which have come down from colonial times, the diamond-shaped figure was cut through, but this weakens the structure, so it is simply indicated here by an offset. The gauge lines on the back and front rails are laid out by running spaces ⅜ and ⅛ inch respectively. In the original, the arms were carved to represent the claws of an animal. The finish is similar to that used on the other pieces described in the special chapter on finishing.

Arm Chair

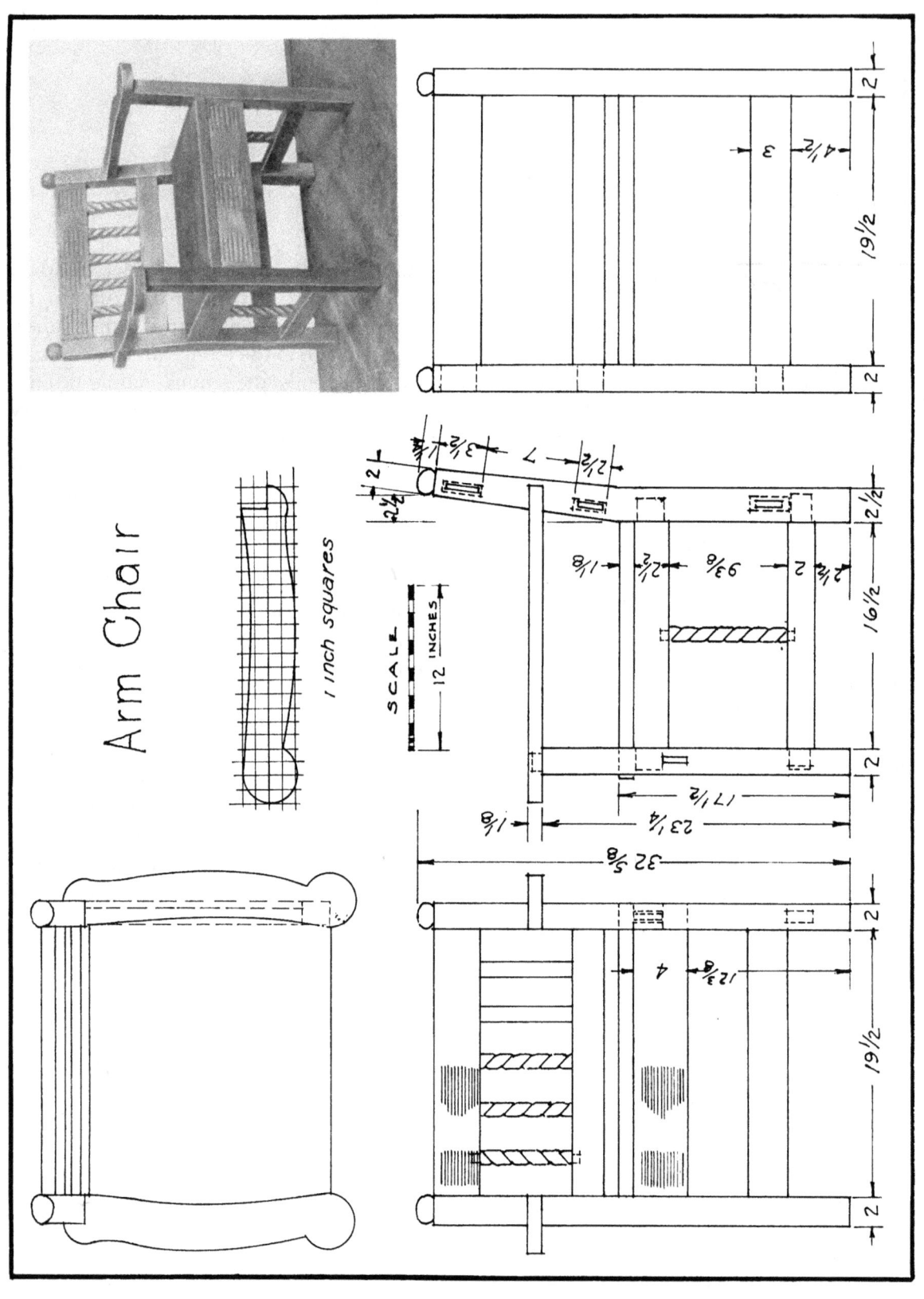

40

Armchair

BILL OF MATERIAL

Pieces

2	2 by 2 by 24	Front legs
2	2 by 4½ by 32⅝	Back legs
2	1⅛ by 4 by 23	Arms
1	1⅛ by 4 by 23½	Front apron
1	1⅛ by 3½ by 23½	Top back
1	1⅛ by 2½ by 23½	Bottom back
1	1½ by 3 by 23½	Lower back stretcher
2	1⅛ by 2½ by 19½	Side rails
2	1⅛ by 2 by 19½	Side stretchers
1	1⅛ by 18¾ by 23½	Seat
5	1⅛ by 1⅛ by 7¾	Back spirals
2	1⅛ by 1⅛ by 10¾	Side spirals

A chair must be comfortable. Also, it must be sturdy, and at the same time it should look well. In designing a chair for strength, there is danger of making it massive and awkward. In the present armchair this danger is overcome by the simple device of carving. The wide rail is broken up by horizontal lines, and spirals lighten the back. This chair can be used in any room of the home.

CONSTRUCTION

In the construction through mortise-and-tenon joints are used except where the side rails and stretchers fit into the back legs. Here blind mortise-and-tenon joints are used so as not to weaken the back legs. All pieces are cut to size, and mortises are cut and put together; then they are taken apart for carving. The front legs are mortised in the arms, fastened with blind wedges, and are pinned from the inside.

CARVING

The spirals for the back are laid out from each corner, so they will run close together. The front rail and back crosspiece are laid out with pencil lines for carving, allowing ⅜ inch for the groove and ⅛ inch between each. The carving is done with a ¼-inch U-shaped carving tool. The knobs are rounded with a flat chisel, but are not sanded. The front legs could be carved. They are heavier than they need be between the seat and the arms.

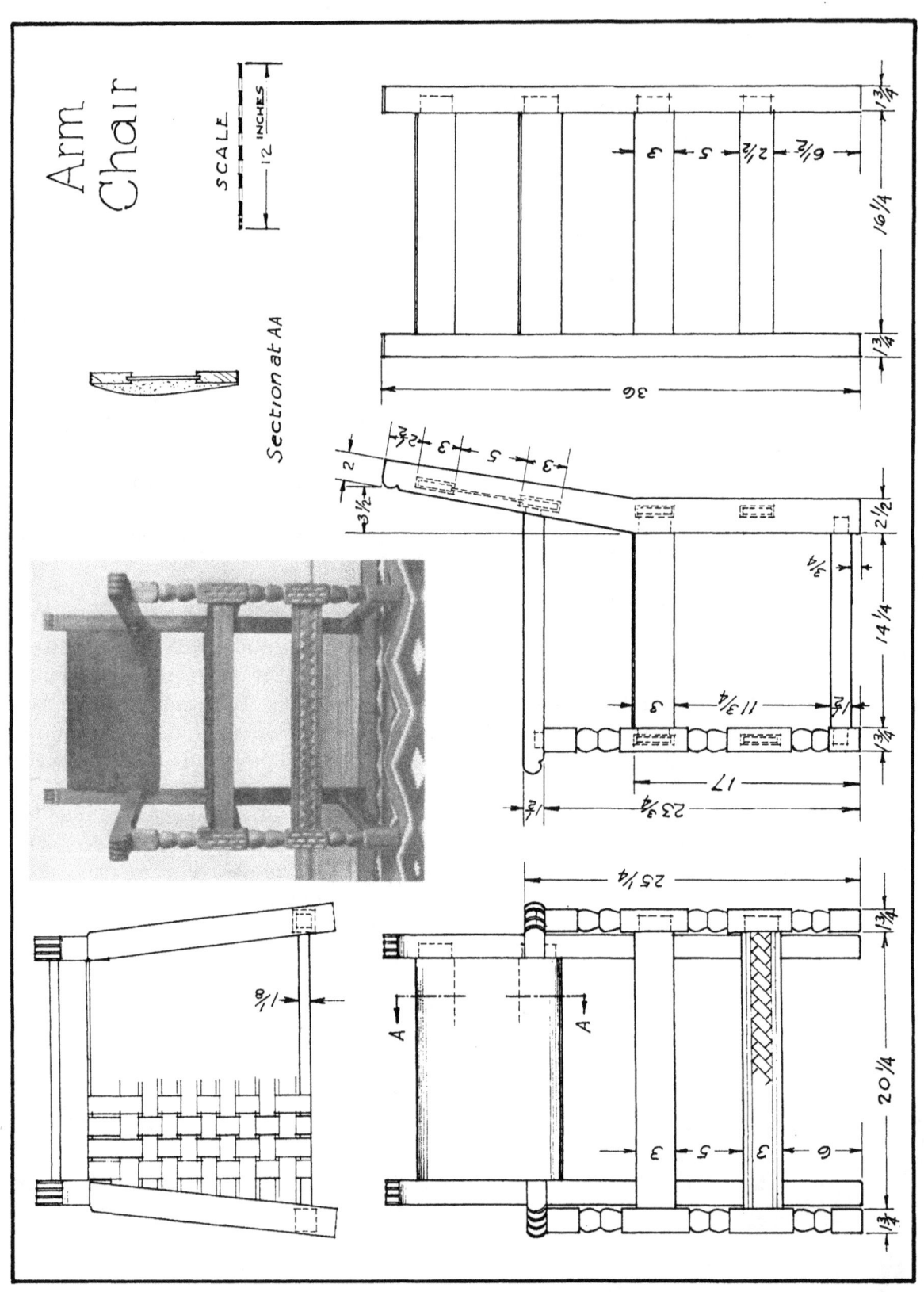

Armchair

BILL OF MATERIAL
Pieces

2	1¾ by 5½ by 36	Back legs
2	1¾ by 1¾ by 24¾	Front legs
3	1⅛ by 3 by 18¾	Back stretchers
1	¼ by 5½ by 16¼	Back panel
1	1⅛ by 2½ by 18¾	Back stretcher
2	1⅛ by 3 by 22¾	Front stretchers
2	1⅛ by 3 by 16¾	Side rails
2	1⅛ by 1½ by 16¾	Side stretchers
2	1½ by 2 by 20	Arms

Braces for corners under seat
Harness leather or rawhide for seat and back
Cotton padding for edges and back

A chair of this type is both artistic and comfortable. It has about it the atmosphere of Old Spain, and is well suited to use in the present-day Spanish-type homes.

CONSTRUCTION

Blind mortise joints are used on this chair, but they are secured with dowel rods. The cutting and fitting must be accurately done; otherwise defects in workmanship will show and the artistic character of the chair will be lowered. Both the rail and the stretcher are necessary on the front because of the heavy pull of the suspended seat.

In the old colonial chairs reinforcement blocks were used beneath the seat, holding the rails securely in place. Sharp edges were padded beneath the leather. Strips for the seat were cut from the rawhide of a cow. The hair was removed from the hide by soaking in a lye solution and scraping. The strips were nailed in place while wet. The back was a solid piece of leather.

In present-day chairs commercial leather can be used where the rawhide is not available. In fastening the leather, ornamental brass-headed nails should be used.

CARVING

The carving is simple. The front legs can be turned on the lathe, or they can be carved by hand. If they are done by hand, the chisel marks should not be sanded out. The front stretcher is done by running a saw kerf 3/16 inch deep, about ½ inch from each edge. By use of the T bevel the center section is broken up into a series of parallelograms. The diagonal lines are cut to a depth of 1/16 inch, and the small triangles are chipped out to the depth of the kerf lines. The back legs and arms are fluted with a ⅜-inch gouge.

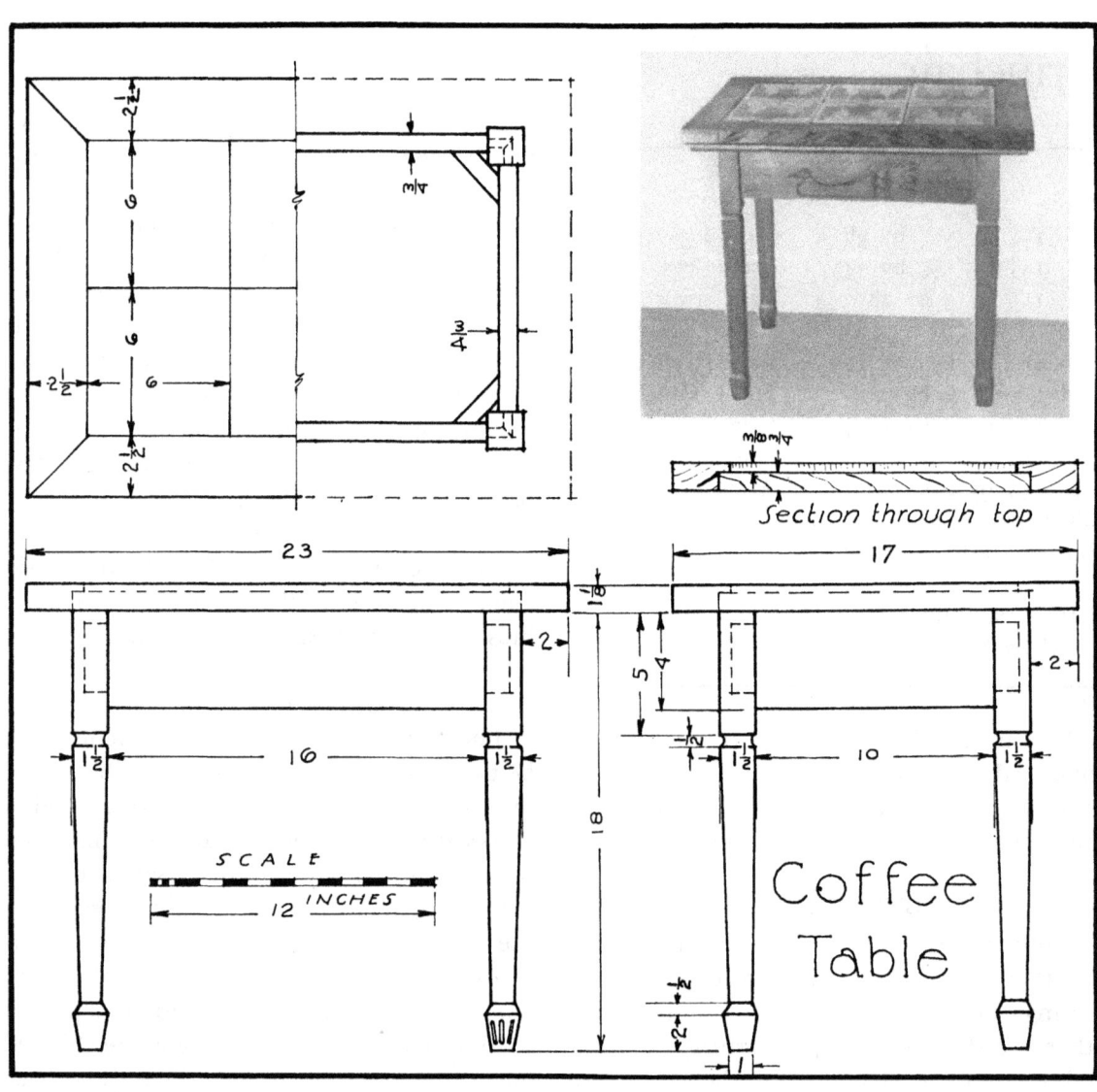

Coffee Table

Coffee Table

BILL OF MATERIAL

Pieces

4	1½ by 1½ by 18	Legs
2	¾ by 4 by 18	Side rails
2	¾ by 4 by 12	End rails
1	¾ by 13 by 19	Blind top
4	¾ by 4 by 3	Braces
2	1⅛ by 2½ by 23	Frame
2	1⅛ by 2½ by 17	Frame
6 tiles, ⅜ by 6 by 6		Top

The coffee table has become an essential piece of furniture in most homes. In colonial times a small, low table of this type was made of wrought iron and tile and was probably used as a bench.

CONSTRUCTION

Blind mortise-and-tenon joints are used. The blind top is of ¾-inch material, and is made flush with the outside of the legs. The frame for the top is made like a picture frame, mitered at the corners and held together with splines. The groove on the back fits over the ¾-inch top, leaving a space ⅜ by 12⅛ by 18⅛ inches for the tile. The tiles measure 6 by 6 inches, and a slight space should be left between them. The top is fastened to the rails with top clips.

CARVING

The carving is not shown in the plate. Either carving or an offset design should be used on the rails to lighten their appearance. In the table shown, the bird on the rail is of Hopi origin. The edge has a series of triangular depressions, painted blue and red. Each of the tiles has a Navajo Thunder Bird painted in orange and black with regular china paints and fired.

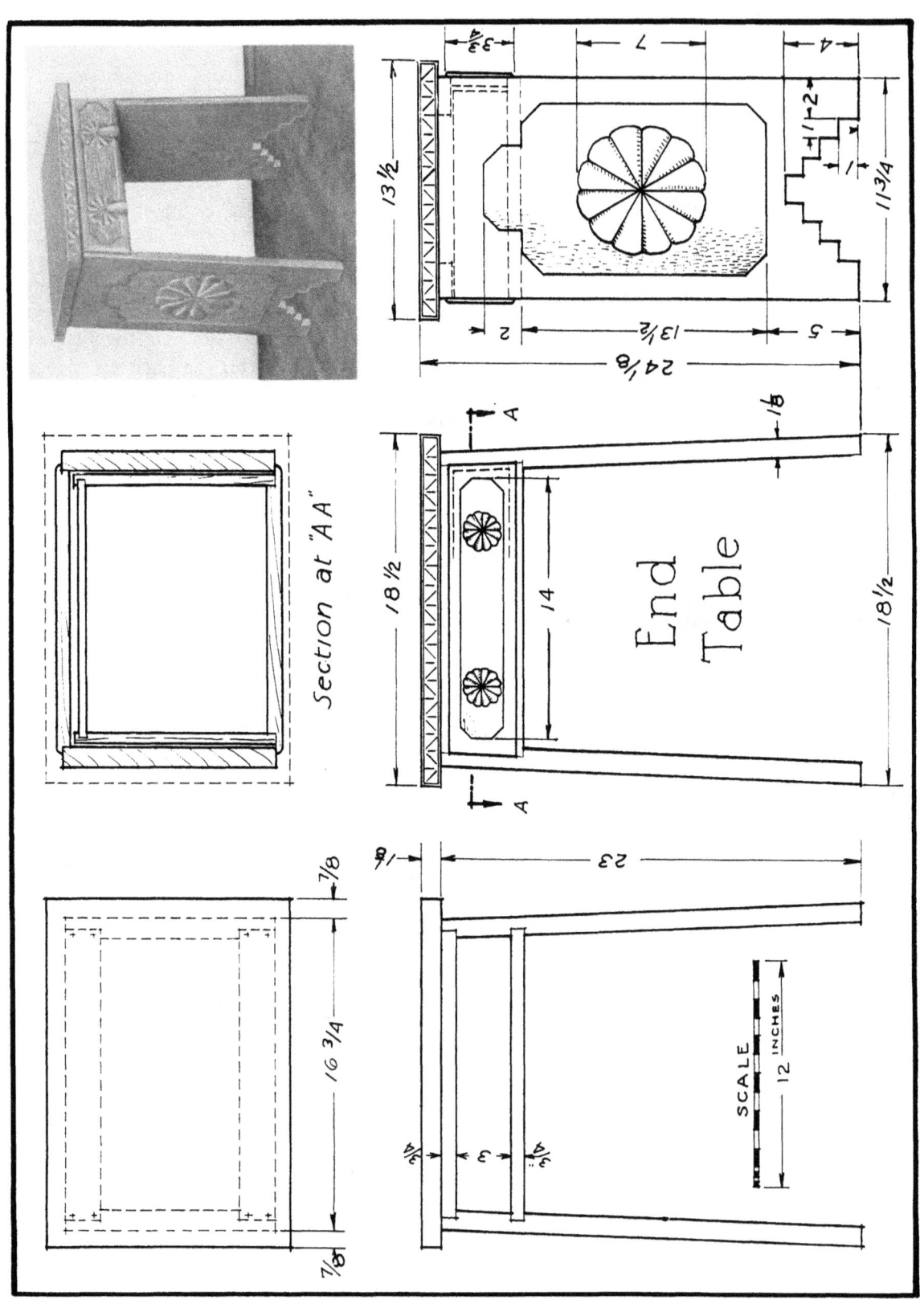

End Table

BILL OF MATERIAL

Pieces

2	1⅛ by 11¾ by 23	Ends
1	1⅛ by 13½ by 18½	Top
1	¾ by 11¾ by 16	Shelf
2	¾ by 2 by 15½	Crosspieces
2	¾ by 3¾ by 16	Drawer front and apron
2	½ by 2⅞ by 11	Drawer sides
1	½ by 2⅜ by 13¾	Drawer back
1	¼ by 11 by 13¾	Drawer bottom

This little table has conservative lines. It can be used in either a living room or a bedroom. In the living room, it may be set against a wall near the fireplace with a small rug under it, and a piece of Pueblo pottery may be placed on top of it. If located at the end of a davenport or along the arm of a chair, it will serve as a smoking stand.

CONSTRUCTION

The two ends are cut from 12-inch stock. If a frame is used for a drawer support, it should be well constructed. A solid shelf can be used as a support. The two end pieces are grooved on the inside to fit the shelf which is glued into position. They are notched to a ¾-inch depth on the inside of the top of the end pieces to take the two crosspieces which are made of two pieces of ¾ by 2-inch stock. The crosspieces should be sufficiently shorter than the shelf so that the right spread may be given to the endpieces. The crosspieces are clamped in position, and both glue and nails are used to hold them in place. The drawer support is held in place with glue only. If a solid shelf is used for a drawer support, ⅝-inch holes are bored through the shelf for the screw driver to reach the screwheads which fasten the top. The top is made of 1⅛-inch material and is fastened to the crosspieces with screws from beneath. The back is the same as the front with the exception of drawer pulls. The backpiece is carved and grooved, and is secured in place by glue and by nails from the top and bottom. This piece helps to support the structure. The drawer pulls can be similar in shape to those of larger pieces of furniture, or they can be a loop of soft leather run through the center of the rosette and nailed on the inside.

CARVING

The designs are the simple rosettes on each endpiece and the two rosettes where the drop pulls are fastened to the drawer. The meander design of chip carving goes completely around the edge of the table top. The back of the table is the same as the drawer front, with the exception of the drop pulls. A piece similar to the drawer front is notched to fit between the crosspieces and the drawer support, and is nailed into position before the top is fastened.

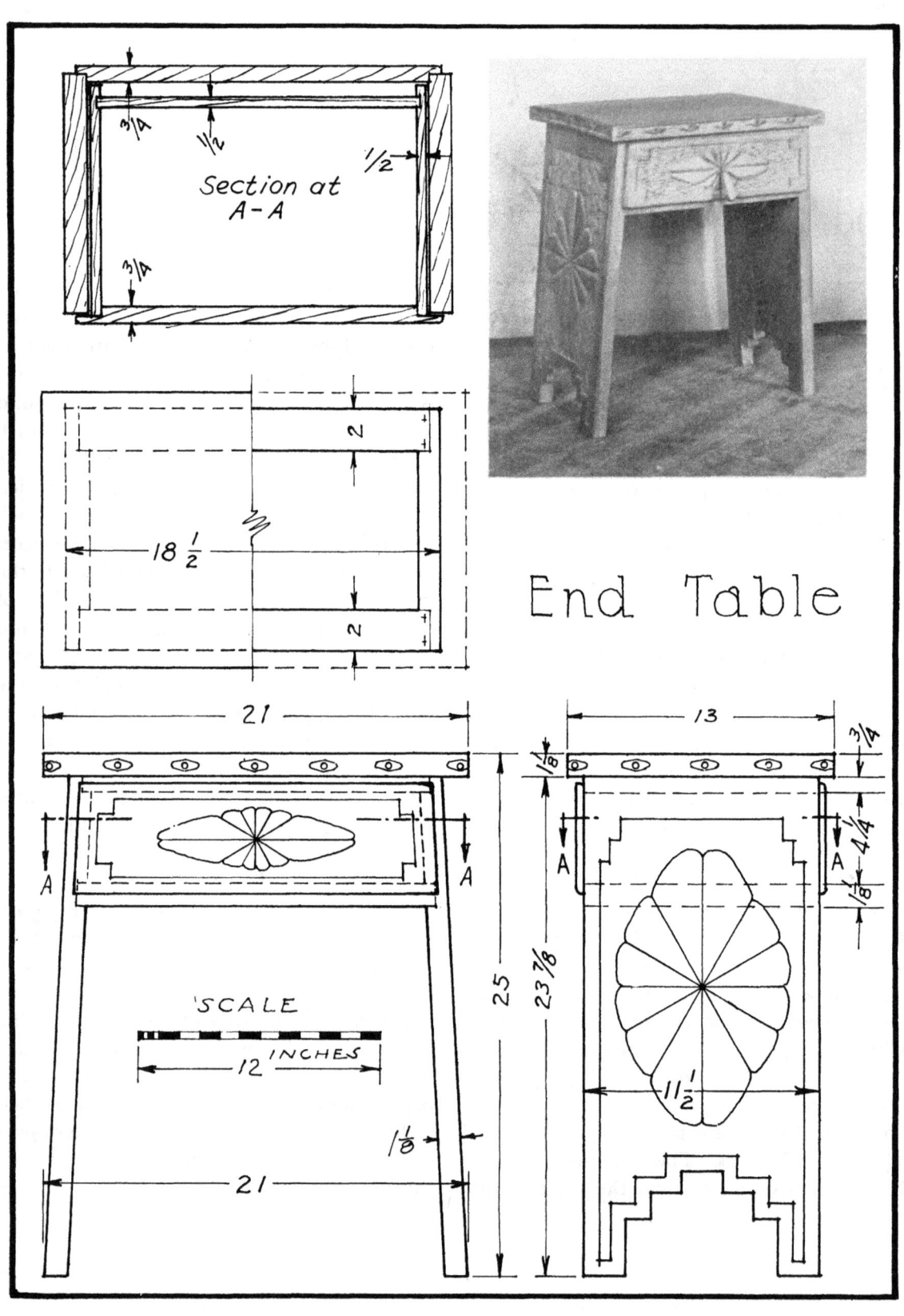

End Table

BILL OF MATERIAL

Pieces

2	1⅛ by 11½ by 23⅞	Ends
1	1⅛ by 13 by 21	Top
1	1⅛ by 11½ by 17	Shelf
2	¾ by 2 by 16	Top stretchers
1	¾ by 5¼ by 17¼	Back panel
1	¾ by 5¼ by 17¼	Drawer front
2	½ by 4¼ by 11	Drawer sides
1	½ by 3½ by 15½	Drawer back
1	¼ by 11 by 15½	Drawer bottom
1	¾ by ¾ by 3	Drawer pull

This end table is similar to others listed, except that it is built of 1⅛-inch material instead of ¾-inch stock. It has a distinct spread to the legs and is more substantial than the other tables.

CONSTRUCTION

The legs are 1⅛ by 11½ by 23⅞ inches. They are grooved to 1⅛ inches wide and ½ inch deep to take a shelf which acts as a drawer support. The top is notched to take ¾ by 2 by 16-inch crosspieces. These are held in place with 1½-inch screws. The top is held on by screws through these crosspieces. Holes are bored through the shelf in order to get to the heads of the screws in the top with a screw driver.

CARVING

The carving is a little different from the other pieces. The rosettes are laid out in the usual way; then the center portion is elongated. The bottom portion of the legs is characteristic. The border of the carving follows this outline at a distance of ⅞ inch. The edge of the top consists of a series of raised portions cut by reversing the ½-inch gouge. A hole is bored ⅛ inch deep in the center of each raised portion by using a special bit made from a small steel cylinder. This leaves a flat bottom in the hole. It is well to practice the boring on a piece of scrap wood until a design is found that fits the piece. This gives a very pleasing effect with the elongated rosette.

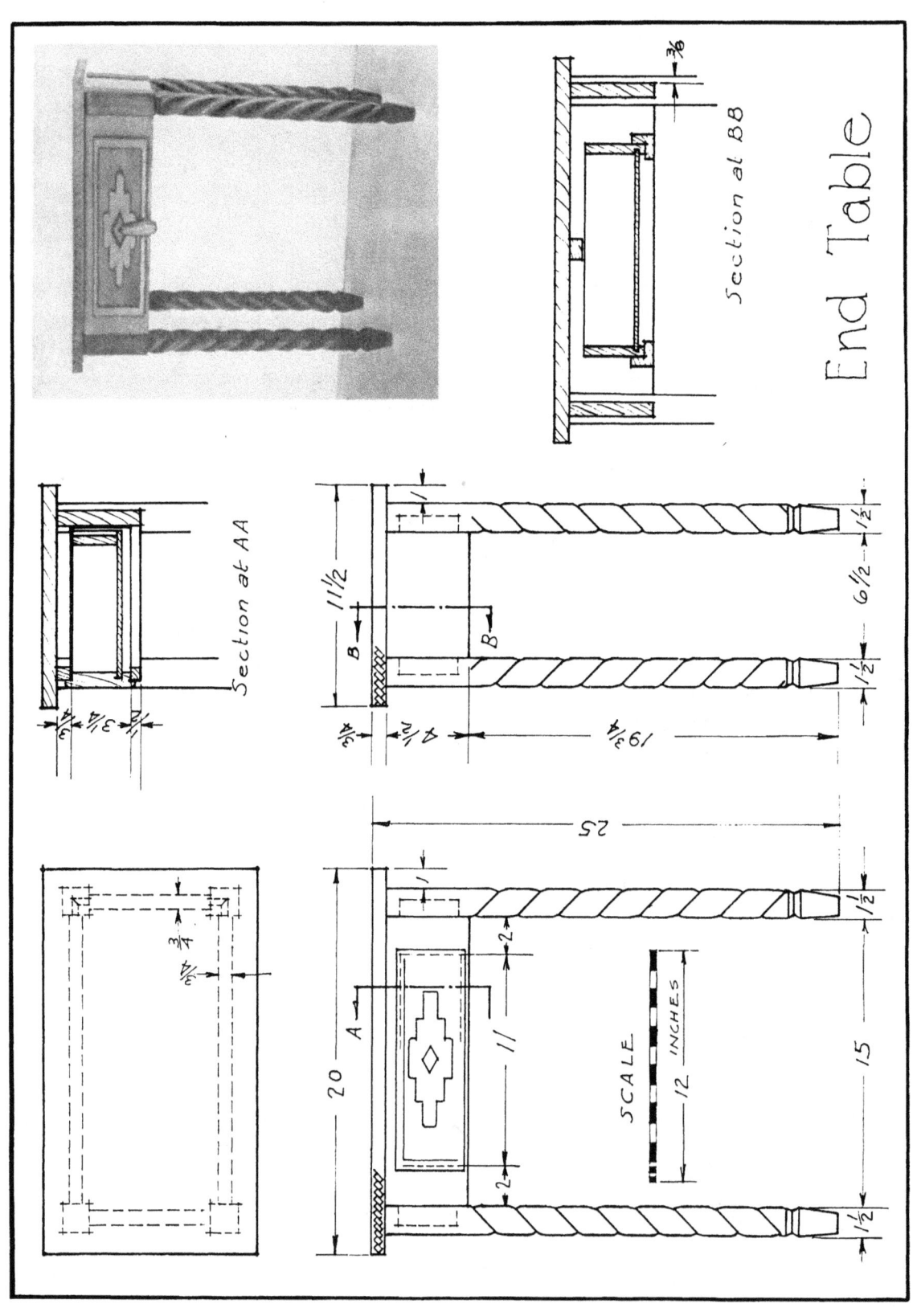

End Table

BILL OF MATERIAL

Pieces			
4	1½ by 1½ by 24¼	Legs
2	¾ by 4½ by 17¼	Side rails
2	¾ by 4½ by 8¾	End rails
1	¾ by 11½ by 20	Top
1	¾ by 3¾ by 11½	Drawer front
2	¾ by 3¼ by 7¾	Drawer sides
1	¾ by 2½ by 10¼	Drawer back
1	¼ by 7¾ by 10¼	Drawer bottom
2	1½ by 1½ by 7¼	Drawer guide
1	¾ by 1⅛ by 6½	Drawer guide

The photograph was taken at an angle which causes the legs to look heavier than they are in reality. The legs are of fir and the rest of the table is pine, so that when finished a two-tone effect results. It is narrow, and may be set close to the wall. It looks well with a piece of Pueblo pottery.

CONSTRUCTION

The joints are blind mortise and tenon. They could be through joints, the tenons each cut away on opposite sides to cross each other in the legs. The opening for the drawer is cut on the jig saw. The plate does not show corner braces, but short braces will strengthen the structure.

CARVING

The offset design on the drawer gives variety. It is raised about ⅛ inch by cutting away the background with a gouge. The fir for the legs does not carve easily, but the grain is exceptionally good. The delicate carving on the edge fits the ¾-inch top.

In finishing, the use of a potassium dichromate solution changes the fir to a dark brown while the pine assumes a light greenish tinge.

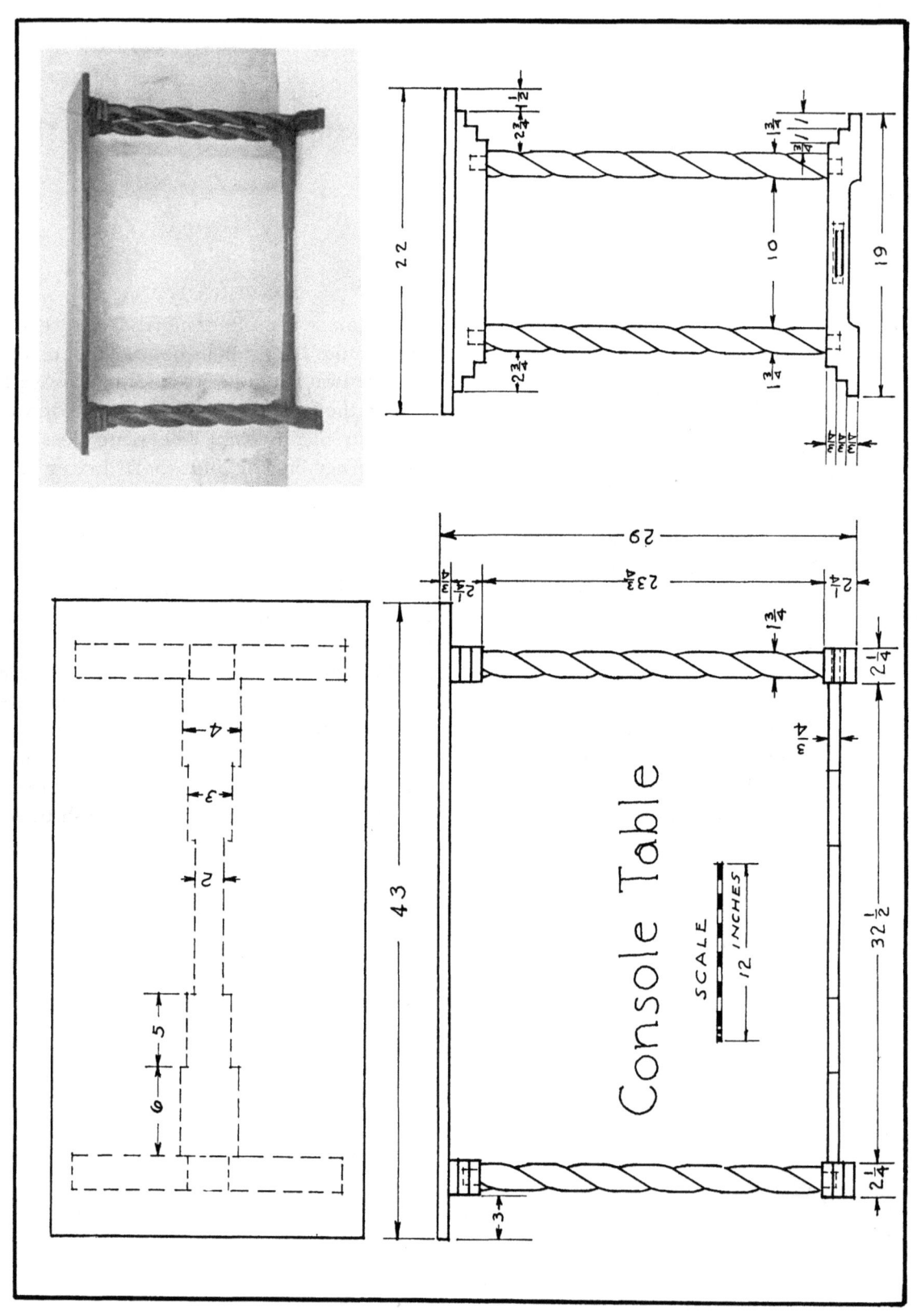

52

Console Table

BILL OF MATERIAL

Pieces
4	1¾ by 1¾ by 26¼	Legs
4	2¼ by 2¼ by 19	Crosspieces
1	¾ by 22 by 43	Top
1	¾ by 4 by 37	Stretcher

This little table is simple to construct and requires very little material. The roped legs take time to carve but the work affords good training for the beginners. The table is long and narrow and fits along the wall of a living room or the back of a davenport. A piece of Pueblo pottery looks well on it.

CONSTRUCTION

The legs are cut to the length indicated, allowing tenons on each end 1¼ inches long. These tenons are pinned with ⅜-inch dowel rods. All crosspieces are cut the same size, and the same step-up design is used. The stretcher is secured in place with a through mortise-and-tenon joint. The table could be strengthened with a stretcher between the top crosspieces. This could be placed on edge or notched into the crosspieces. The top is fastened on with regular top clips.

CARVING

Illustrations for carving the legs are provided in the special chapter on carving. There is no other carving. The edge of the top could be carved, if desired.

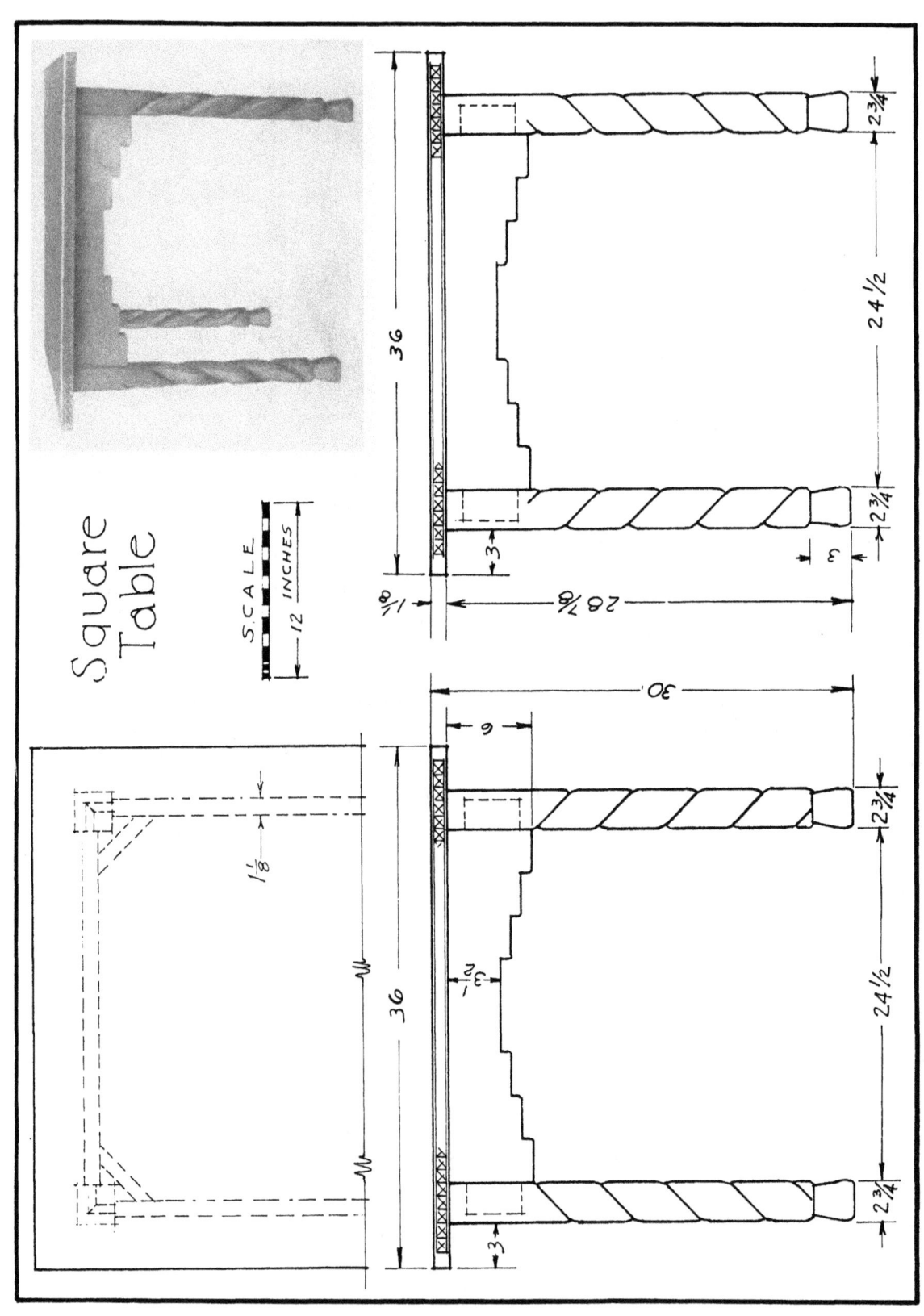

Square Table

Square Table

BILL OF MATERIAL
Pieces
4	2¾ by 2¾ by 28⅞	Legs
4	1⅛ by 6 by 28½	Rails
4	1⅛ by 6 by 7	Braces
1	1⅛ by 36 by 36	Top

The square table is not very practical for the average home. It is used extensively in Spanish restaurants, tearooms, and hotel dining rooms. A number of these tables were constructed for a study room in a girls' boarding home. The table would be excellent in an open-air patio.

CONSTRUCTION

There are very few problems of construction in this project. The tenons on the rails should be made as long as consistent. In the plate, they are shown to be 2 inches long, and are beveled to fit inside the mortises of the legs. The top is glued up with dowel pins or tongue-and-groove joints. Each corner is braced. The top is fastened with regular top clips rather than with screws set in the rail.

CARVING

The spirals are cut in the usual way, as described in the special chapter. The length of the feet should be about 3 inches for this size leg. The offset on the rails is about ¾ inch, but it may vary. The object is to lighten the appearance of the rail without weakening it.

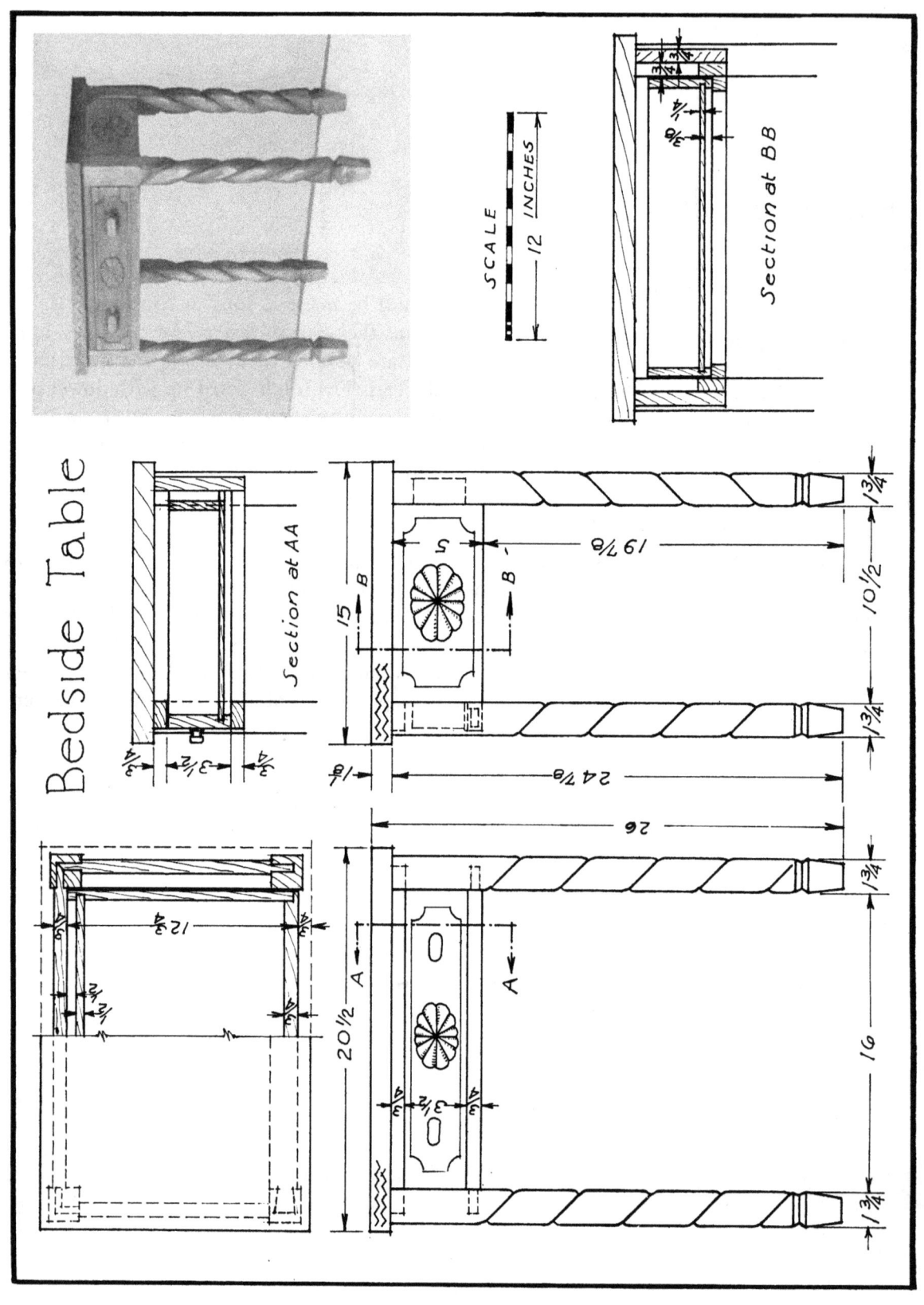

Bedside Table

BILL OF MATERIAL

Pieces		
4	1¾ by 1¾ by 24⅞	Legs
2	¾ by 5 by 13	End rails
1	¾ by 5 by 18½	Back rail
2	¾ by 1½ by 18½	Top and bottom stretchers
2	¾ by 1½ by 10½	Drawer guides
2	¾ by ¾ by 11	Drawer supports
1	1⅛ by 15 by 20½	Top
1	¾ by 3½ by 16	Drawer front
2	¾ by 3½ by 12½	Drawer sides
1	½ by 2⅞ by 15¼	Drawer back
1	¼ by 12½ by 15¼	Drawer bottom

The present-day bedside table has developed from the ancient candlestand. Originally it held a candle for reading; later it held an oil lamp; and still more recently it carries an electric lamp. With modern lighting its utility has not vanished. Now it supports the novelty cigarette dispenser, accommodates the ashes that miss the ash tray, and proudly sustains the extension telephone. It is strong enough to carry its owner when he replaces a light bulb or when he tries to reach the top shelf in the clothes closet.

CONSTRUCTION

Blind mortise-and-tenon joints are used, except for the crosspiece above the drawer. On this piece a dovetail half-lap tenon is used in the tops of the legs. The drawer support is mortised into the legs with a tenon, but should be reinforced by a piece attached to the inside of the legs with screws.

CARVING AND DESIGN

The spiral leg is well adapted to this table. It lightens the appearance while still retaining the strength of the leg. The elongated rosette gives interest to the wide rail. Knobs are used instead of drop pulls, but these, of course, are optional. The edge carving is easy to lay out and execute. This table is about right for a typewriter, but if used for that purpose the drawer should not be as deep as shown.

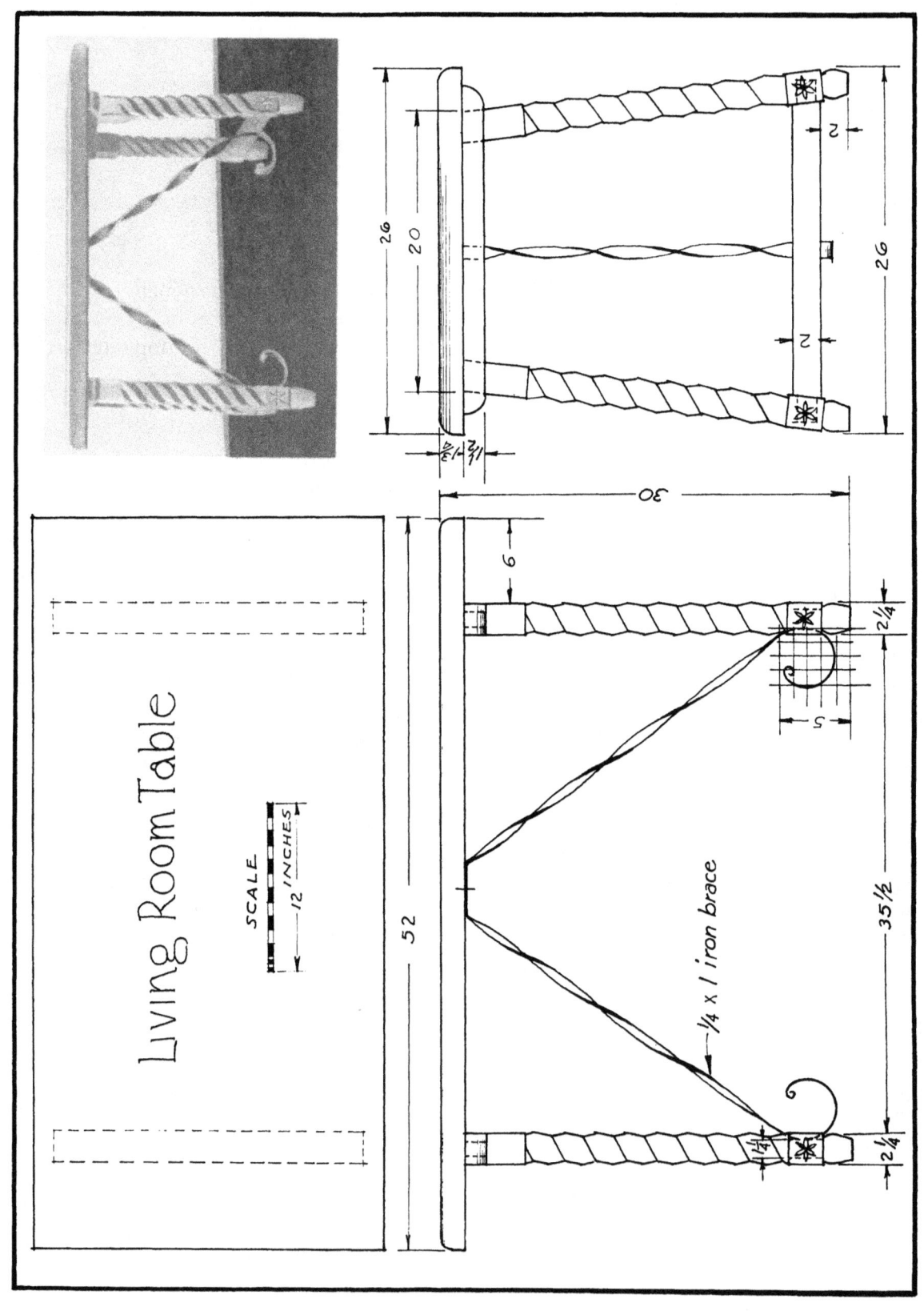

Living-Room Table

BILL OF MATERIAL

Pieces

4	2¼ by 2¼ by 28½	Legs
2	1¼ by 2 by 24	Stretchers
2	1½ by 2¼ by 24	Crosspieces
1	1¾ by 26 by 52	Top
1	¼ by 1 by 90	Iron for brace

A table of this type has many commendable features. It is especially heavy and sturdy in construction. The top is 1¾-inch material; the legs also are heavy.

CONSTRUCTION

The legs are cut to size, marked for the stretcher and top tenons, and then laid out for carving. The two legs are placed on the workbench to get the desired spread, and the T bevel is set for the angles. The tenons on the stretchers are cut 1¾ inches long. The tenons on the tops of the legs should reach through the crosspieces. The iron brace is fastened to the stretcher by lag screws or bolts reaching through the stretcher. The weight of the stretcher, as indicated in the plate, should be 1¼ by 2 inches.

CARVING

The carving on the legs is not rounded as much as usual. The grooves travel from each corner, running the spirals close together. The six-pointed design is carved on the three sides of each leg. It is a simple star laid out with the compass. The top is rounded on the upper edge, but no carving is used. The stretchers could be carved on the outside.

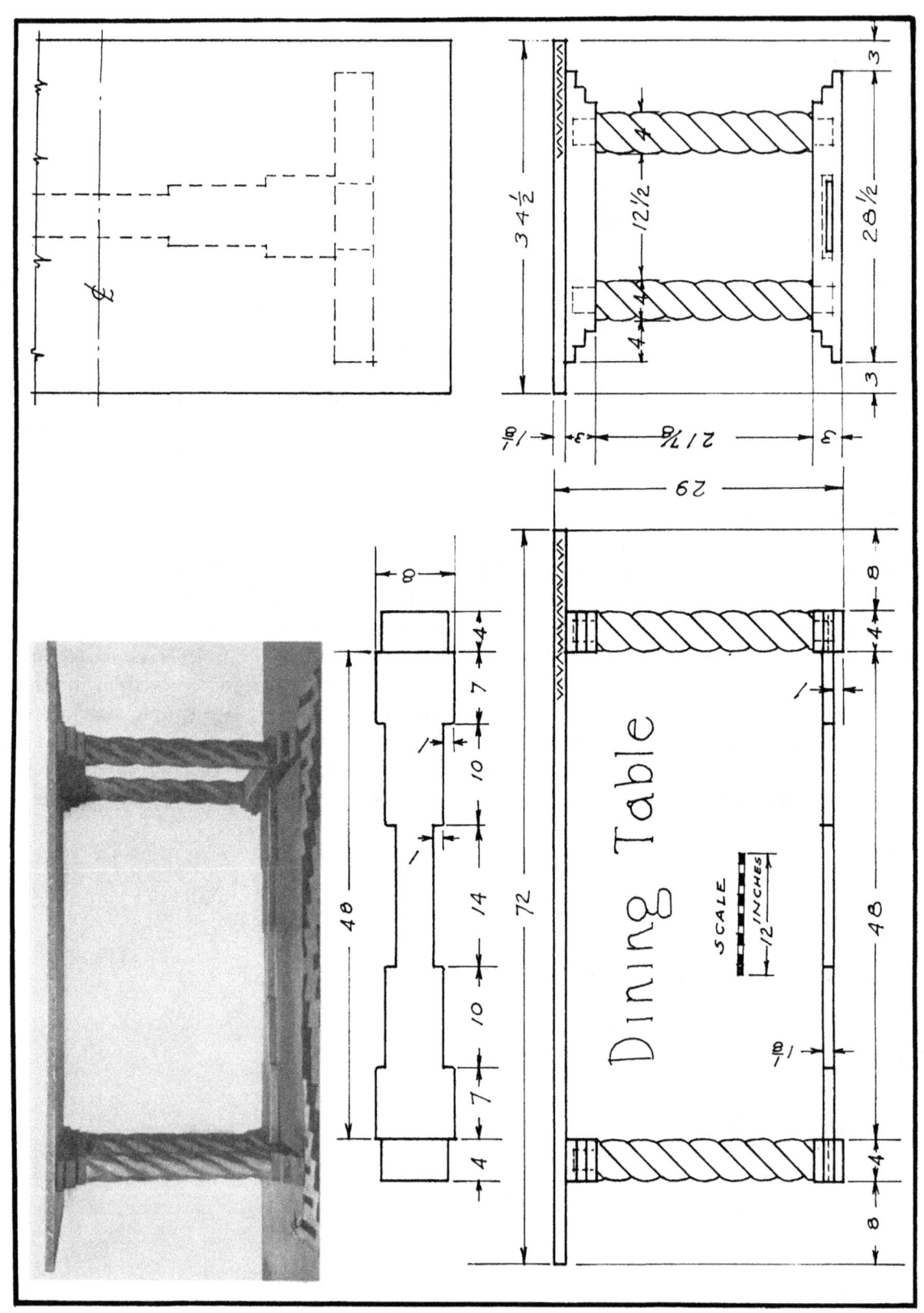

60

Dining Table

BILL OF MATERIAL

Pieces
- 4   4 by 4 by 25¾   Legs
- 4   3 by 4 by 28½   Crosspieces
- 1   1⅛ by 8 by 56   Stretcher
- 1   1⅛ by 34½ by 72   Top
- 4   3/16 by 2 by 5   Strap iron

This large table can be used in the living room as well as in the dining room. It also makes a distinctive, useful piece of furniture for the library or the classroom. The crosspieces and legs are made of clear grade lumber. The top should be made of D select or better. The stretcher should be made wide with a thick tenon so as to act as a brace.

CONSTRUCTION

Full 4 by 4-inch stock should be used for the legs. The stock is cut to length for legs, and tenons are laid out on each end. The tenons reach almost through the crosspieces and are made heavy. They are glued and pinned with ½-inch dowel rods. The lower crosspieces have a through mortise for the stretcher.

Each end is glued up as a unit and tested for squareness. After the glue sets, the two ends are assembled by gluing the stretcher in place. The stretcher tenons are pinned from beneath with two pins on each end. A temporary piece is nailed across the top to hold the two ends in place, while the glue sets.

Instead of using the regular top clips, four pieces of strap iron are cut 3/16 by 2 by 5 inches and mortised into the top crosspiece 1 inch from each end. Elongated holes are cut on each end to hold the top in place. This holds the top more rigid and helps to brace the table.

CARVING

This was one of the earlier experimental tables constructed in the shop. The spirals all run in one direction. They also run close together, a rope or ridge starting from each corner. The offsets on the crosspieces are square. The appearance of the piece can be improved by rounding these. The meander design on the edge is explained in the special chapter. It is easily done and takes very little time.

Dining Table

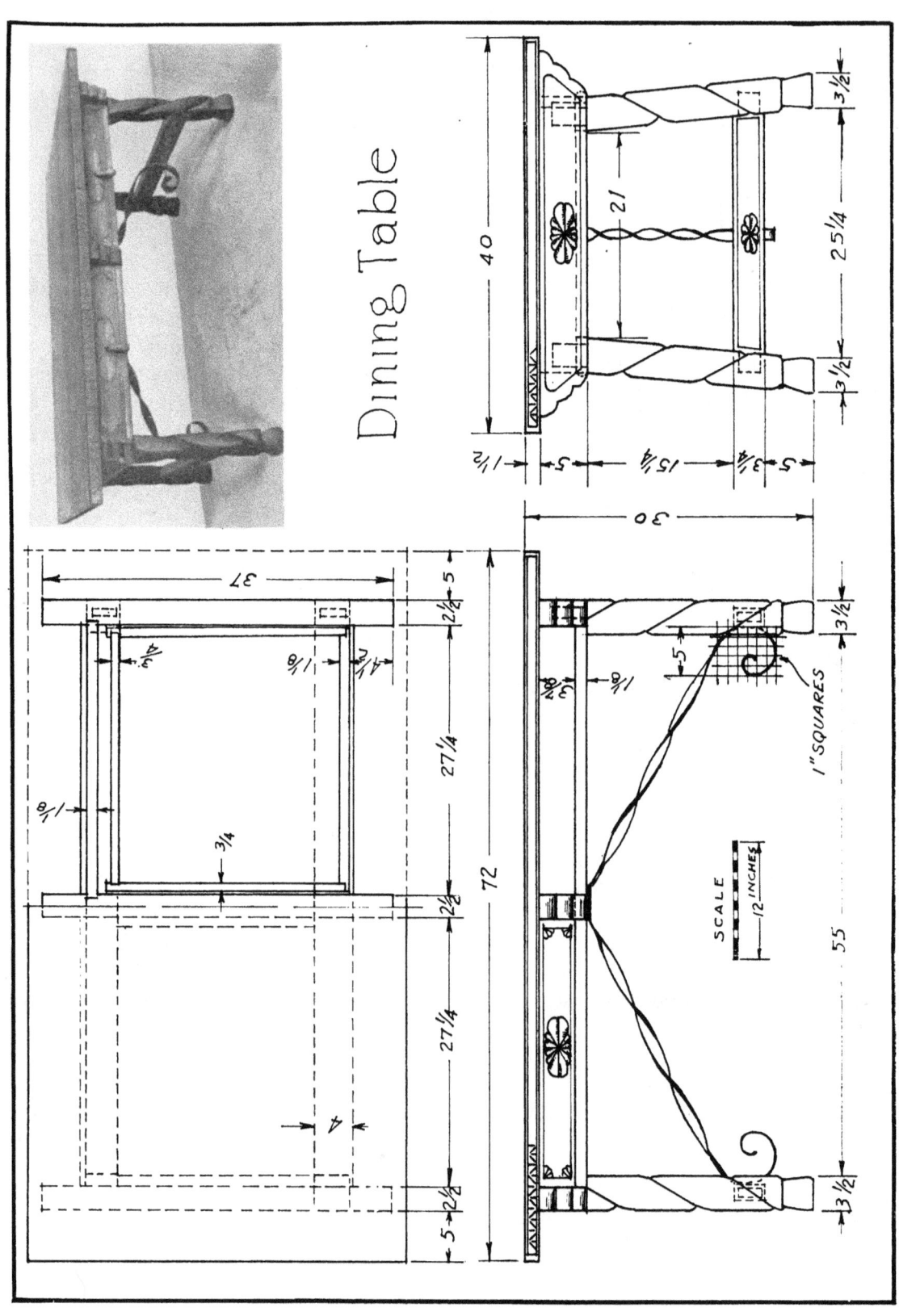

Dining Table

BILL OF MATERIAL

Pieces		
4	3½ by 3½ by 29	Legs
3	2½ by 5 by 37	Crosspieces
1	1½ by 40 by 72	Top
2	1⅛ by 4 by 59	Stretchers
2	1⅛ by 3⅞ by 27¼	Panels
2	1⅛ by 3⅞ by 27¼	Drawer fronts
4	¾ by 3⅞ by 26	Drawer sides
2	¾ by 3⅜ by 26	Drawer backs
2	¼ by 26 by 26	Drawer bottoms
2	1½ by 3¼ by 29¼	End stretchers
1	3/16 by 2 by 100	Iron brace

This sturdy table may be built of relatively low-grade material. It takes a small amount of stock. The style is in the spirit of the early Spanish colonial. The spiral carving of the legs is found on heavier pieces of old Spanish colonial furniture but was not often employed on smaller pieces. Wrought-iron braces may take the place of the more commonly used wood stretcher.

CONSTRUCTION

The legs are cut from 4 by 4-inch stock. They are 29 inches long, the tenons at the upper ends reaching almost through the crosspieces. The crosspieces which are 2½ inches thick are cut from 3-inch stock. The tenons are made as large as possible. To get the angle for the tenon, the two legs are laid on the top of the bench in position to get the right spread. The T bevel is set, which will also indicate the angle on the end stretchers. As in the case of the leg tenons, the tenons on the stretchers are made as heavy as possible. Mortises are cut and assembled with glue. All joints are secured with pins. The two ends are thus assembled as units.

Instead of using the mortise-and-tenon joint on the legs, a cross-lap joint, which is more practical, may be used.

The top has tongue-and-groove joints. It is held in place with table-top clips. If the top clips are not available, the screw holes are elongated in the crosspieces to allow for expansion.

CARVING

All pieces are carved before assembling. The tenons should be marked for cutting before the legs are carved, and after carving they may be cut. The meander design on the edge of the top is done by taking out alternate clips on each side of a center section. Details of laying out this edge are covered by a special chapter. The spirals on the legs are not carved very deeply. The panels on both sides of the table are the same except that the drawer fronts have drop pulls. A design on each end is similar to that on the front.

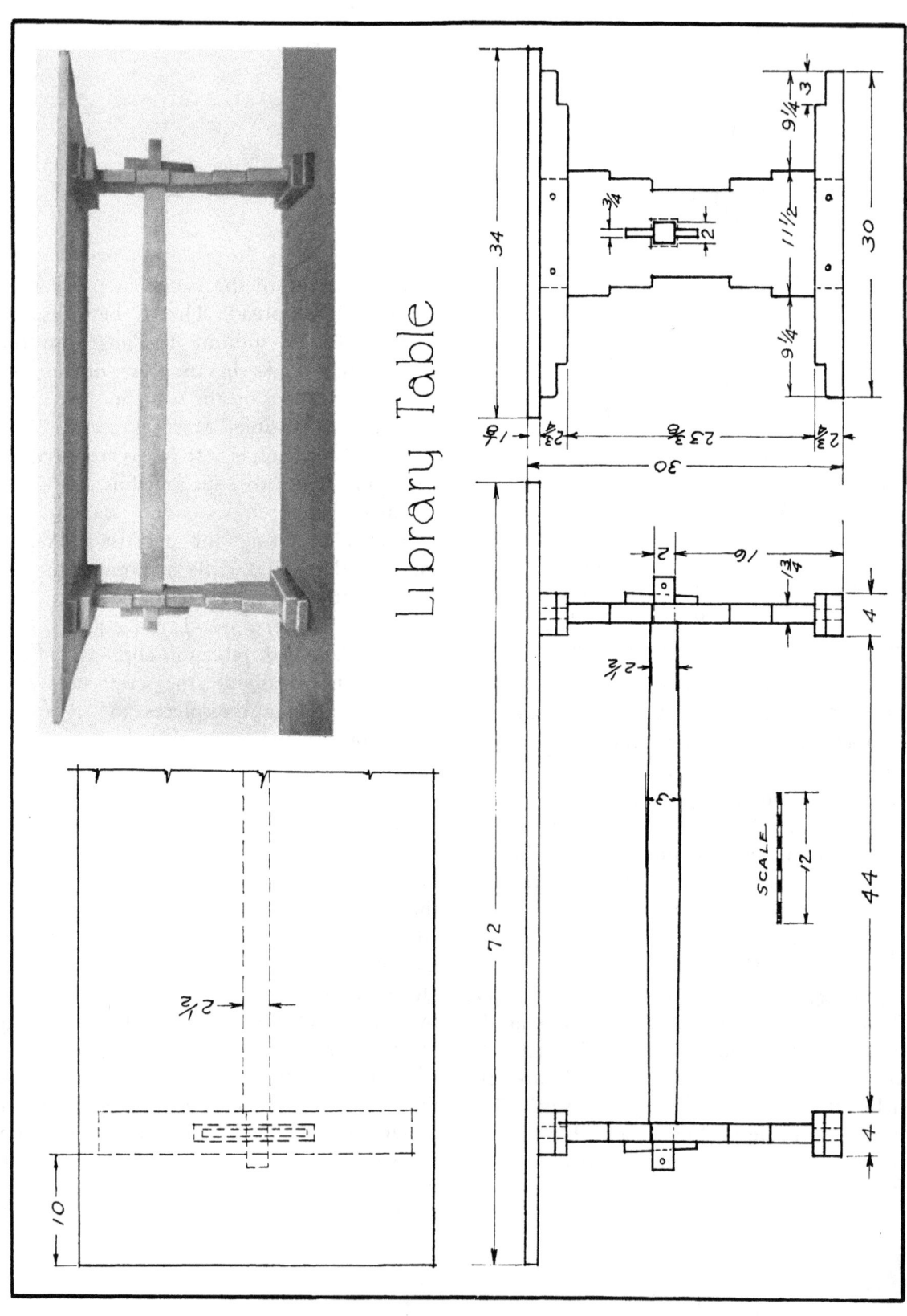

Library Table

Library Table

BILL OF MATERIAL

Pieces
2	1¾ by 11½ by 28⅞	Ends
4	2¾ by 4 by 30	End crosspieces
1	2½ by 3 by 58	Stretcher
2	¾ by 1¼ by 9	Oak pins
1	1⅛ by 34 by 72	Top

The outstanding features of this table are its simplicity of structure, strength, and cheapness of material. The top is made of D select and the remaining parts are No. 2 shop material. The table has plain, simple lines, and is made of heavy material. It is a suitable living-room or library table, and can be used in the dining room if made 40 or 42 inches wide.

CONSTRUCTION

The two ends are cut to size from 2 by 12-inch stock. The tenons should reach through the endpieces. The ends are mortised to fit, and each joint is glued, and is pinned with ½-inch dowel pins. Each end is assembled and glued up as a unit. Each end then is tested with a square and rule to see that the clamps have not pulled the parts out of line. The mortise for the stretcher calls for careful work with the chisel. The mortise is laid out before the pieces are cut to shape, so that they will be square with the shoulders of the tenons. The stretcher is made of 2¾-inch stock in order to get a sufficient shoulder to hold the ends rigid. The wedge pins are made of hardwood. The holes for the wedges are cut so the ends can be wedged against the shoulders of the stretcher. The top is fastened on by the use of 3/16 by 1½ by 5-inch iron plates, and countersunk in the top crosspieces. The screw holes are elongated at the ends of the plates to allow for contraction.

DESIGN

No carving is used on this table, although the edges of the top could be carved. The offset ends are rounded with chisel or cabinet file. This type of table can be knocked down quickly for transportation or storage, and can be reassembled in a few minutes.

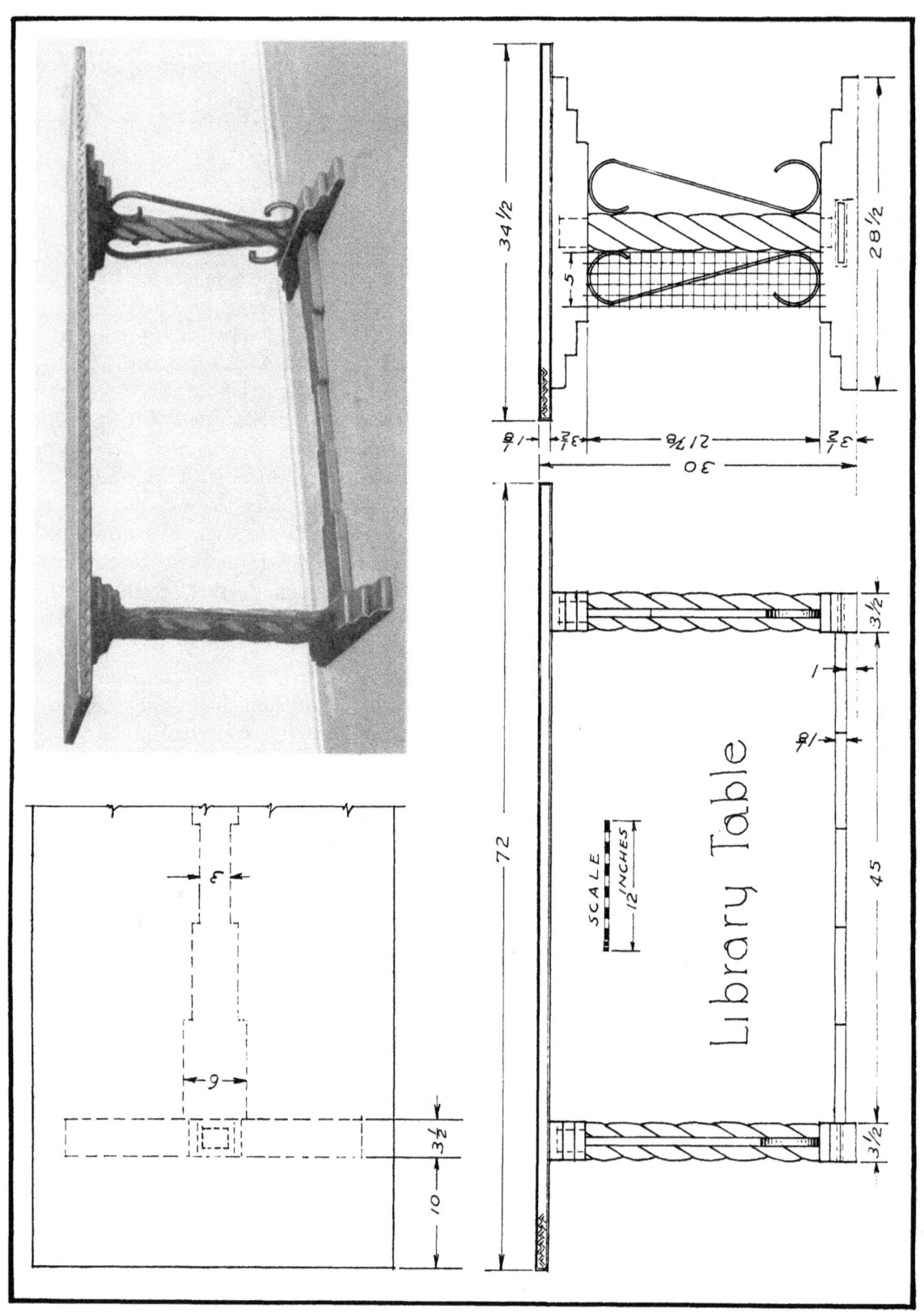

Library Table

Library Table

BILL OF MATERIAL

Pieces		
2	3½ by 3½ by 25⅞	Legs
4	3½ by 3½ by 28½	End crosspieces
1	1⅛ by 6 by 52	Stretcher
1	1⅛ by 34½ by 72	Top
4	¼ by 1 by 40	Wrought-iron braces

This distinctive table has pleasing lines. It is quite often used as a dining table, but it is a little narrow for that purpose. The wrought-iron braces strengthen the structure and make it attractive. The crosspieces and legs are made of common-grade lumber so the cost of material is minimized.

CONSTRUCTION

While 3½ by 3½-inch stock is shown in the drawings, full 4 by 4-inch stock may be used for the legs to increase their size and improve their appearance. The stock is cut to length for the legs, and the tenons are laid out on each end. The tenons reach almost through the upper crosspieces and are mortised 1½ inches into the lower crosspieces, to allow the stretcher to be mortised through them and to be pinned from beneath. The four crosspieces are uniform in layout. The spirals are carved and mortises are cut in the crosspieces.

The two ends should be glued up without the stretcher. They should be clamped together and checked to be sure that the crosspieces are perpendicular to the legs, and that both ends are exactly the same. The joints are pinned with dowel rods, and the wrought-iron braces are fastened in place with 1½-inch lag screws. When the stretcher is glued in place and pinned, the structure is ready for the top.

Instead of using the regular top fasteners, four pieces of strap iron are cut 3/16 by 2 by 5 inches and mortised into the top crosspieces 1 inch from the ends. Elongated holes are cut on both ends to attach to the top. This will hold the structure rigidly and will allow for the expansion of the top.

CARVING

The spirals on the legs run close together, the ridge starting from each corner. The offsets on the crosspieces and stretcher are well rounded and sanded to give the characteristic feather effect. The meander design of the edge is explained in the special chapter. It is easily done and takes very little time.

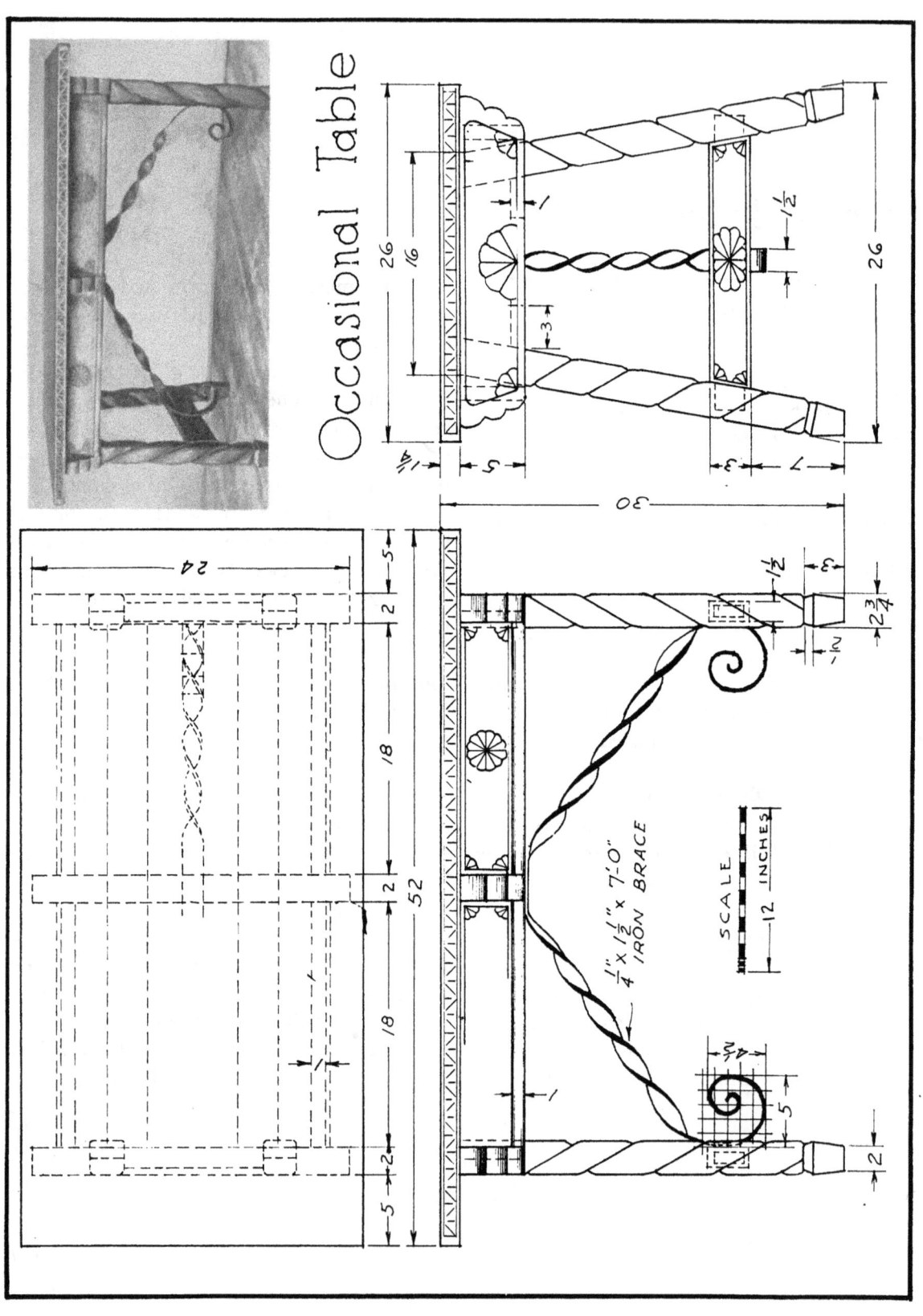

Occasional Table

Occasional Table

BILL OF MATERIAL

Pieces		
4	2¾ by 2¾ by 29	Legs
3	2 by 5 by 24	Crosspieces
1	1¼ by 26 by 52	Top
2	1 by 3 by 40	Stretchers
4	1⅛ by 5 by 18	Side panels
2	1½ by 3 by 21½	End stretchers
1	3/16 or ¼ by 1½ by 84	Iron brace

This table is designed to fit into a convenient place in the living room. Usually it is placed along a wall. It is sometimes constructed with two drawers and drop pulls similar to a large living-room table. When placed in a den, it serves well as a magazine table.

CONSTRUCTION

The elements of construction in this table are quite simple, the assembling of the two ends being the only difficult operation. The legs are cut to the dimensions indicated and are clamped together in a vise. A rule is laid on them and dimensions are marked off for feet and crosspieces at the top. Then, starting with the line showing the upper edge of the groove on the foot, equal spaces of 2¾ inches are marked off for the part that is to be carved. The legs then are taken out of the vise, and these lines are run around each leg, beginning at the line where the lower portion of the part is to be carved, and running diagonal lines on all four sides of the legs. These diagonals will run to the right on two legs and to the left on the other two. The same angle is kept on the short segments at the top. The marking gauge then is set at ⅜ inch, and lines are run on all corners of the parts to be carved. Then alternate diagonals are cut with a backsaw to a depth of ⅜ inch.

It is best to take a black pencil and mark well the diagonals that are not to be cut before sawing the first one. With a sharp chisel a cut is made with the grain of the wood toward the saw kerf. A V-shaped groove then is cut out to the bottom of the saw kerf and about ⅝ inch on each side of the kerf. As yet the grooves do not come together on the corners which are beveled to the ⅜-inch lines. The groove is joined across the corners with a sharp carving knife, and with a wide chisel it is worked to the desired rounded shape.

It is better to lay out the tops of the legs for the crosspieces and cut the mortise for the stretchers before doing any carving. The stretchers are fitted into place and are scribed so that this portion of the leg will not be carved. It will be easier to hold the legs in the vise if the top cross lap is not cut until after the carving is done. The crosspieces for the ends are cut about 1 inch deep to fit the legs, leaving them flush on the outside. The crosspieces are notched on the inside to take the stretchers.

CARVING

A 1-inch chisel ground to a long bevel makes a good tool for shaping the legs. If a knot is encountered, a regular chisel and mallet can be used. The legs are left slightly square or can be rounded as desired. The feet can be changed as desired. On the crosspieces the design is raised by cutting away the background with a carving tool or gouge. The figures can be varied to fit the space. The geometric design on the edge of the top is chip carving and is done with a knife or a specially ground chisel. Before doing the carving, it is well to practice on a piece of scrap wood until the desired depth of carving is found.

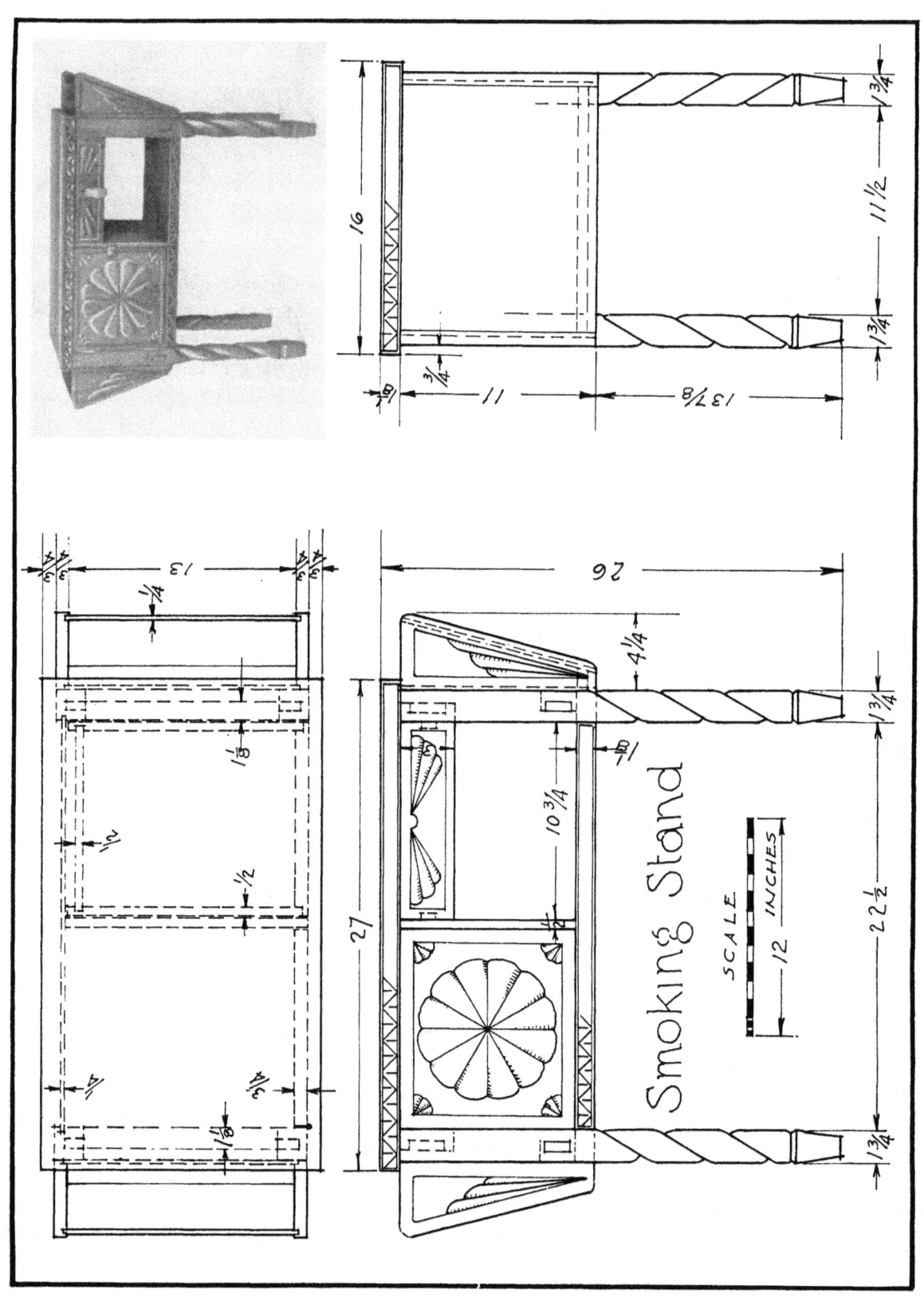

Smoking Stand

BILL OF MATERIAL

Pieces		
4	1¾ by 1¾ by 24⅞	Legs
4	¾ by 4½ by 11	Magazine-pocket sides
1	1⅛ by 15 by 29½	Bottom
1	1⅛ by 16 by 27	Top
2	1⅛ by 3 by 14	Top rails
2	1⅛ by 2 by 15	Bottom rails
1	½ by 15 by 9⅞	Partition
1	¾ by 9⅞ by 11	Door
1	¼ by 9⅞ by 23	Back panel
1	¾ by 3 by 10¾	Drawer front
2	½ by 3 by 13¾	Drawer sides
1	½ by 2¼ by 9¾	Drawer back
1	¼ by 9¾ by 13¾	Drawer bottom
4	¼ by 13½ by 11	Magazine-pocket panels
2	¼ by ½ by 13	Drawer guides

A combination of smoking stand and magazine table is a handy piece of furniture at the side of the easy chair. It is convenient, easily moved, and fits into the environment of the modern Spanish home.

CONSTRUCTION

The four legs are cut to size. They are mortised to take the crosspieces, grooved ¼-inch to take the inside panels of the magazine pockets, and to take the sides of the magazine pockets. These sidepieces are grooved for the ¼-inch panels of the pockets and then are glued to the four legs. The bottom is notched to fit the legs, leaving the bottom extend on each end to serve as bottom for the magazine pockets. It is fastened in position by using screws to the crosspieces. The closed compartment has doors on both sides, and the drawer has a panel on the back the same as the front, so the table is the same on both sides. The feet are a departure resembling the Italian.

CARVING

The carving on the magazine pockets is similar to that on the drawer ends. The background is cut away with a gouge, leaving the figure in relief. The figure is well rounded with a chisel and is sanded smooth to bring out the grain of the wood. The exposed edges of the top and bottom are chip carved.

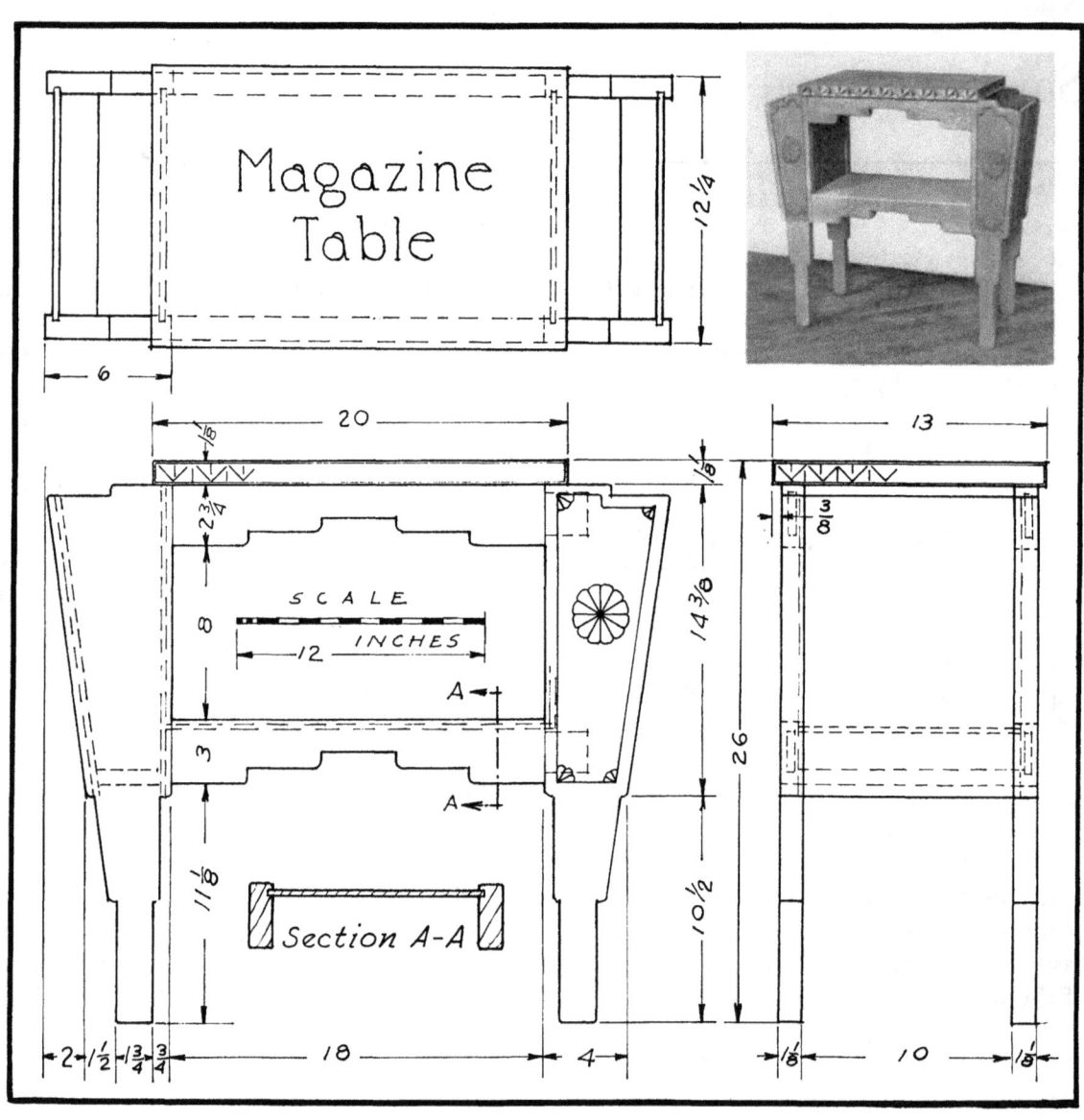

Magazine Table

BILL OF MATERIAL

Pieces		
4	$1\frac{1}{8}$ by 6 by $24\frac{7}{8}$	Legs
2	$1\frac{1}{8}$ by $2\frac{3}{4}$ by 22	Upper rails
2	$1\frac{1}{8}$ by 3 by 22	Lower rails
4	$\frac{1}{4}$ by $10\frac{1}{2}$ by $14\frac{3}{8}$	Pocket panels
1	$\frac{1}{4}$ by $10\frac{1}{2}$ by $18\frac{1}{2}$	Shelf
2	$\frac{3}{4}$ by 3 by $10\frac{1}{2}$	Pocket bottoms
1	$1\frac{1}{8}$ by 13 by 20	Top

While this magazine table is a departure from existing ancient pieces, it is designed to follow the lines of Spanish period furniture. It is small, compact, and well balanced. The two pockets and shelf furnish three distinct compartments, so that any magazine can be readily found. It can be used as an end table in either den or living room.

CONSTRUCTION

The four legs are made from $1\frac{1}{8}$ by 6 by 25-inch pieces. These legs are so shaped that they can be grooved on the saw to take the $\frac{1}{4}$-inch plywood for the pockets. The lower stretchers are grooved $\frac{1}{4}$ inch inside to make the $\frac{1}{4}$-inch panel for the shelf flush with the top of them. Glue is used in the grooves for the pocket panels. All gluing is done in one operation. The structure must be checked carefully for squareness. After the glue has set, the panel of the shelf is notched to fit the legs, and nailed into place with brads. Four pieces of stock, 1 inch square, are cut to fit between the stretchers, two of them to support the shelf and the other two to hold the top in place.

CARVING

The top is carved on the sides and ends with a geometric design, and each of the legs is decorated with a small rosette. All carving is done before assembling the parts. Various Indian symbols have been used to advantage in designing the legs.

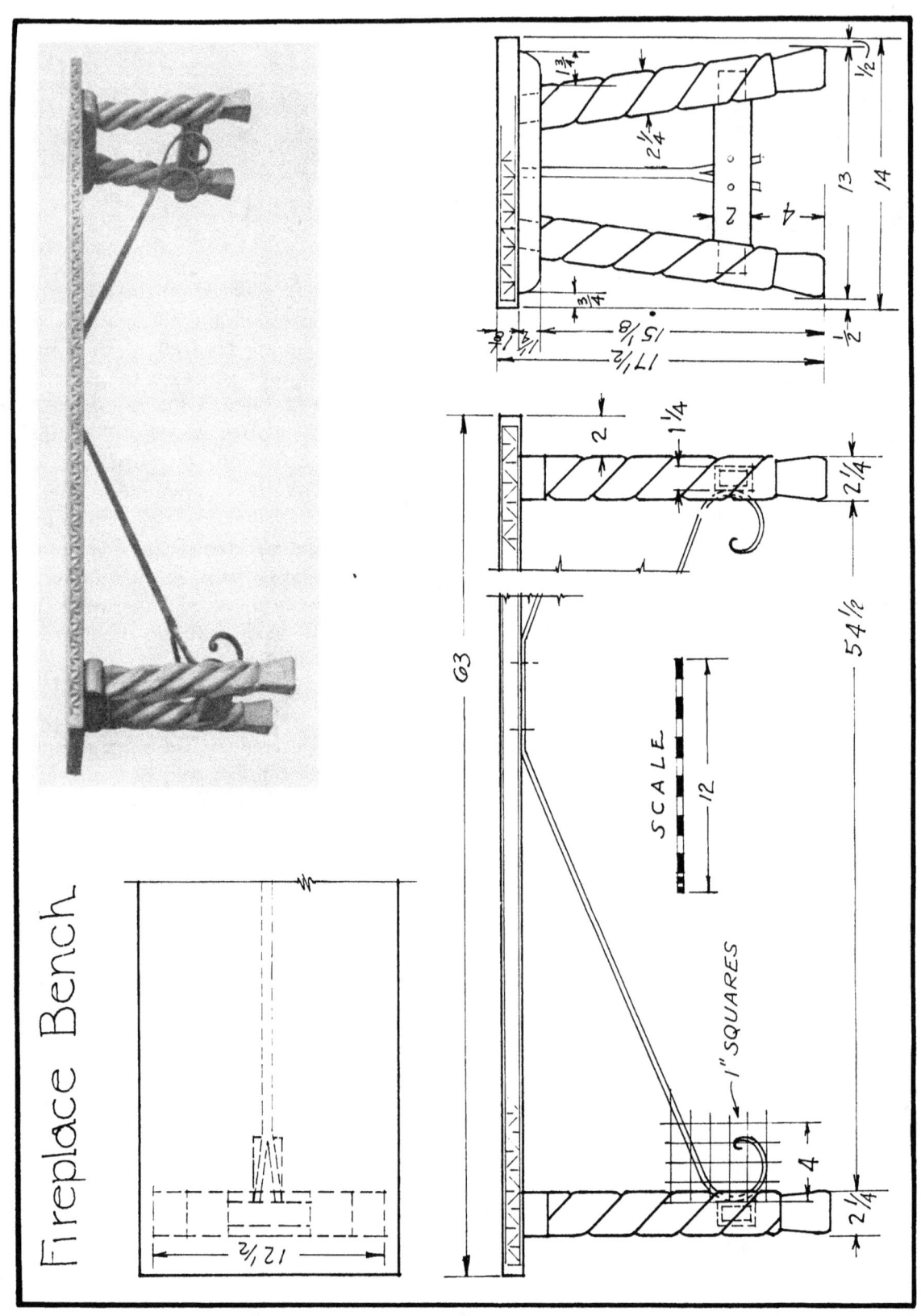

Fireplace Bench

Fireplace Bench

BILL OF MATERIAL

Pieces

4	2¼ by 2¼ by 17	Legs
2	1¼ by 2¼ by 12½	Crosspieces
2	1¼ by 2 by 11½	Stretchers
1	1⅛ by 14 by 63	Top
1	¼ by 1 by 74	Iron brace

This simple bench is a general utility piece. It is found in the dining room, the living room, and the patio. It is not heavy and can easily be moved from the patio to the fireplace or the kitchen. No Spanish home is complete without a bench of this type.

CONSTRUCTION

The four legs are cut to size, allowing tenons to reach through the top crosspieces, and pinning them when assembled. The two legs are placed on the workbench, and are adjusted to the spread desired. The angle is fixed with a T bevel. This angle then is used to cut the tenons on the stretchers. The two ends are glued up at the same operation so that they will be identical in size. The wrought-iron braces are split so that they will brace each leg separately. They are attached at two places on the stretchers with lag screws. This holds the structure rigid and at the same time gives it a very attractive appearance.

CARVING

The carving on the legs should be done after mortises and tenons are cut so as to allow a flat surface where the stretchers join the legs. In carving the spiral, the grooves are run from each corner. The chip carving should be done around the entire edge of the top.

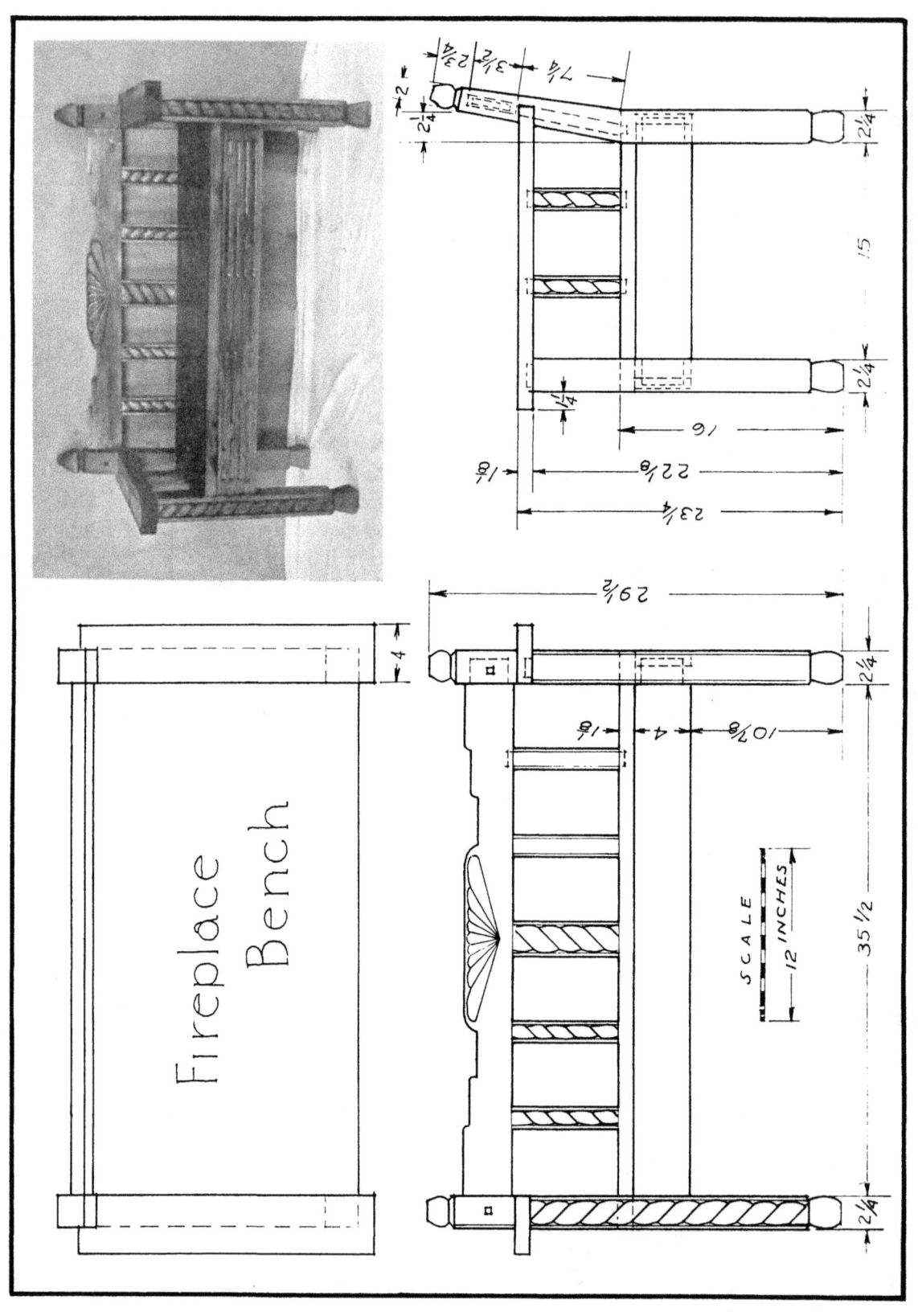

Fireplace Bench

Fireplace Bench

BILL OF MATERIAL

Pieces

2	2¼ by 2¼ by 22⅞	Front legs
2	2¼ by 4¼ by 29½	Back legs
2	1⅛ by 4 by 38½	Side rails
2	1⅛ by 4 by 18	End rails
1	1⅛ by 3½ by 38½	Headpiece
4	1⅛ by 2 by 8¼	Back uprights
1	1⅛ by 3 by 8¼	Back center upright
4	1⅛ by 2 by 7⅛	End uprights
2	1⅛ by 4 by 21½	Arms

The usual fireplace bench is built without a back; however, the old Spanish bench usually had a low back. This is a heavy piece of furniture, but is small enough to be readily moved from fireplace to patio or wherever it is needed. This bench is often constructed with a woven rawhide seat.

CONSTRUCTION

The joints are blind mortise and tenon, but the tenons are long and are pinned to secure them in place. The uprights on the back and sides are cut to length with ½-inch tenons. The back is clamped together and mortises are marked on the back legs. The tenon on the front rail should be offset to accommodate the side rails. The feet are 2½ inches long.

CARVING

The carving is indicated in the plate. The figure on the back is raised by cutting away around it. The spiral effect is produced on the legs and backpieces by rounding the corners of the raised figures.

Patio Bench

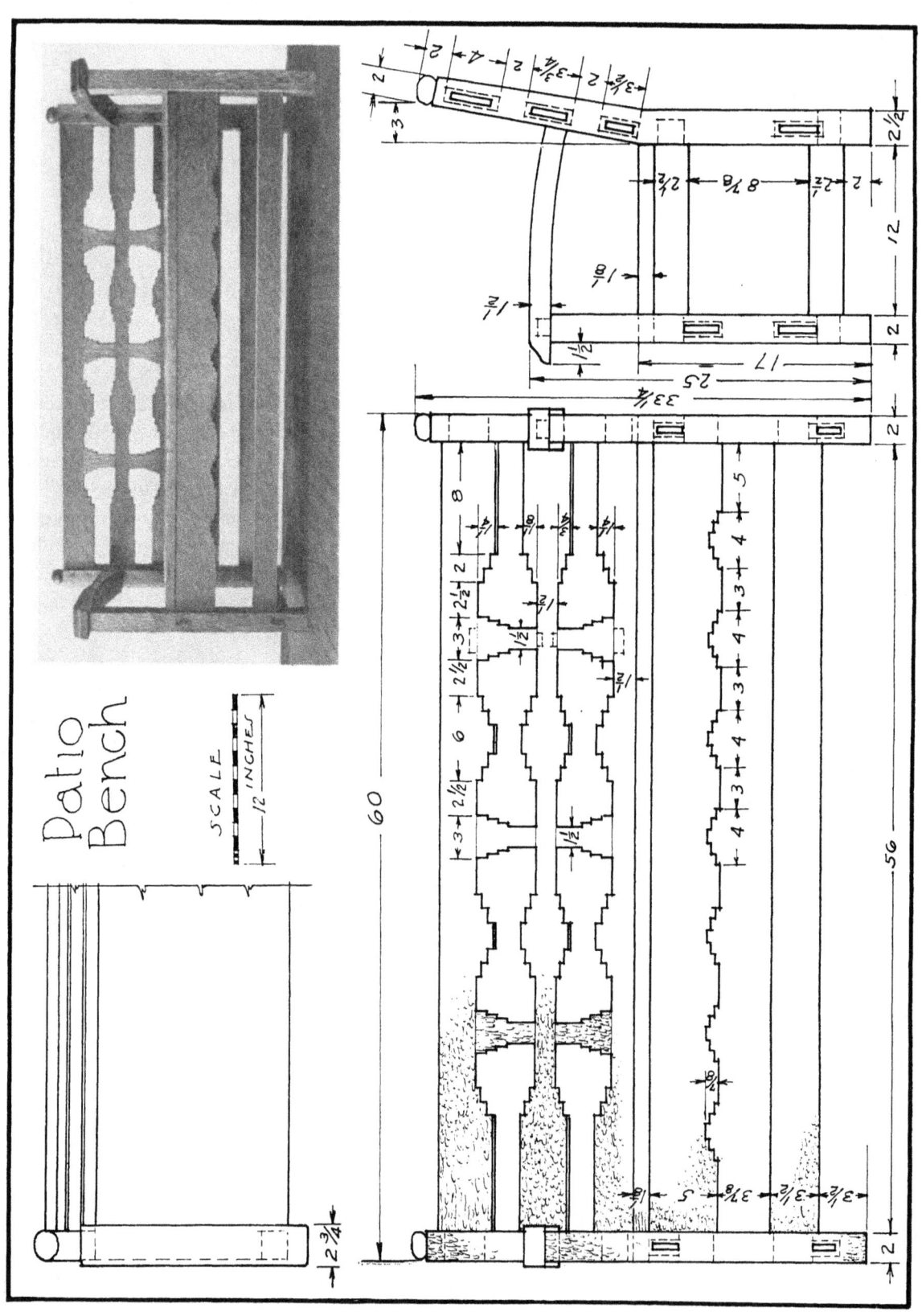

Patio Bench

BILL OF MATERIAL

Pieces		
2	2 by 5 by 33¼	Back legs
2	2 by 2 by 24¼	Front legs
2	1⅛ by 3½ by 60	Back crosspieces (lower)
1	1⅛ by 3¾ by 60	Back crosspiece (middle)
1	1⅛ by 4 by 60	Back crosspiece (upper)
1	1⅛ by 5 by 60	Front crosspiece (upper)
1	1⅛ by 3½ by 60	Front crosspiece (lower)
2	1⅛ by 2½ by 16	End rails
2	1⅛ by 2½ by 16½	End stretchers
2	3 by 3½ by 18	Arms
1	1⅛ by 14 by 60	Seat
3	1⅛ by 3 by 5⅜	Slats
3	1⅛ by 3 by 5	Slats

The Spanish colonial bench was a distinctive piece of furniture. There were many variations in the decoration. This particular type of offset plot has come down from early colonial times. It has distinguishing quality that blends with adobe walls, projecting vigas, and flagstone paved patio.

CONSTRUCTION

Through mortise-and-tenon joints are used. All parts are made to fit before the designs are worked in. The backpieces are laid out. In making the backpieces, use ⅜ to ½-inch offset, depending on their width. A ¼-inch offset on the uprights would be sufficient. All joints are glued and secured with dowel rods. Square pins are more appropriate. The seat is notched to fit the front legs so it will be flush with the front rail; placing the arms in position is the last operation. They are pinned with a dowel pin or are secured with a hidden wedge. To secure a blind mortise-and-tenon joint, the length of the bottom of the mortise is made about 3/32 inch longer than the opening. A saw kerf is made the full length of the tenon and is fitted with a wedge. When the tenon is forced into place the wedge will be forced into the saw kerf and thus will spread the end of the tenon to fit the mortise. With short stub tenons two wedges should be used.

CARVING

The complete front of the bench is carved with a ¾-inch gouge. No figures are used in the decorative scheme. The carving can be varied to suit the individual taste.

Patio Bench

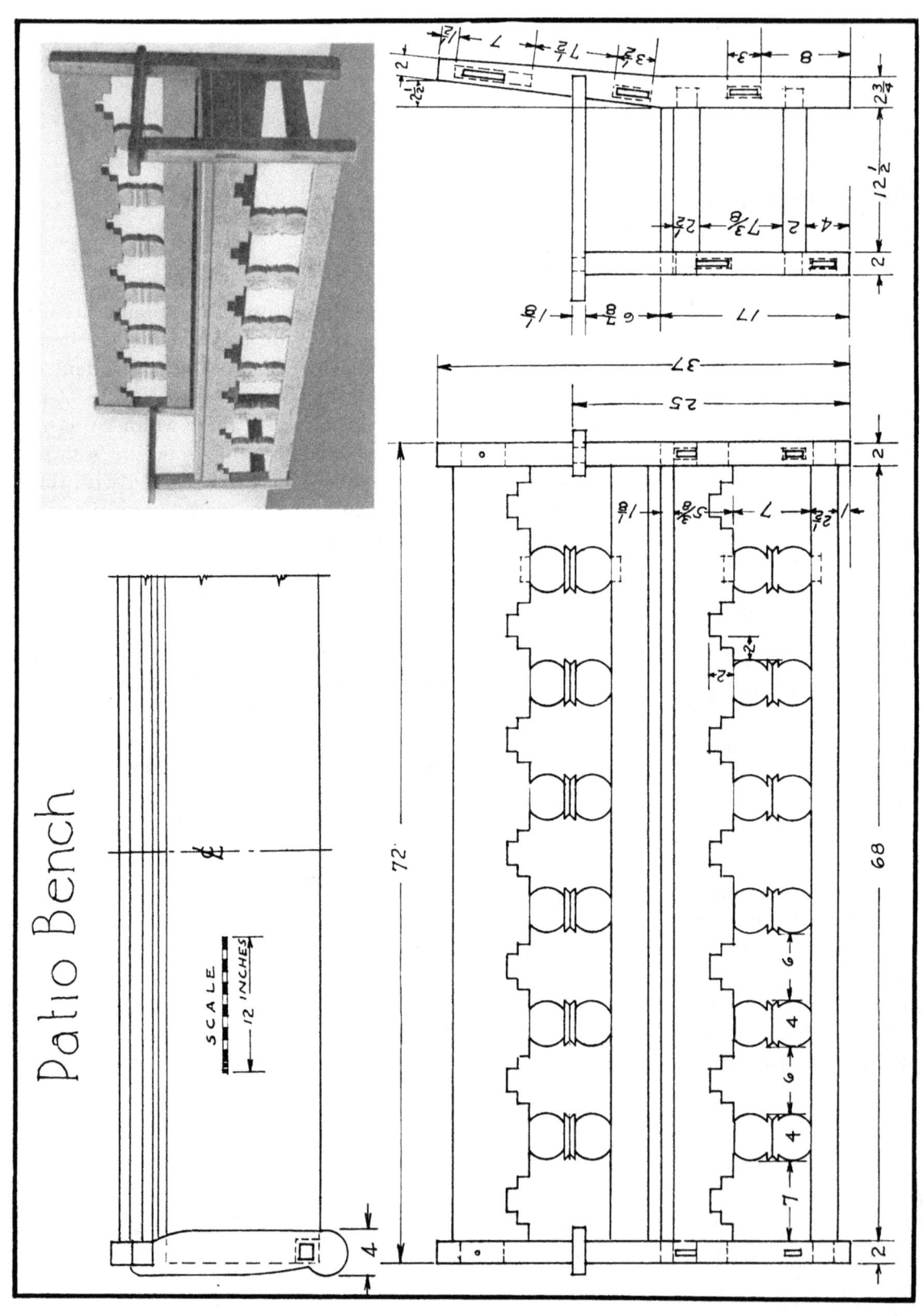

80

Patio Bench

BILL OF MATERIAL

Pieces		
2	2 by 2 by 25	Front legs
2	2 by 4½ by 37	Back legs
1	1⅛ by 5⅜ by 72	Front rail
1	1⅛ by 2½ by 72	Front stretcher
1	1⅛ by 3 by 72	Back stretcher
1	1⅛ by 3½ by 72	Lower back rail
1	1⅛ by 7 by 72	Upper back rail
2	1⅛ by 2 by 16½	End stretchers
2	1⅛ by 2½ by 16½	End rails
2	1⅛ by 4 by 20¼	Arms
6	1⅛ by 4 by 8	Lower fretwork
6	1⅛ by 4 by 8½	Upper fretwork
1	1⅛ by 14½ by 72	Seat

This particular type of bench found much favor during the Spanish colonial period. As a rule it was placed on the long, covered porch facing the patio, but it could also be used in a large living room. Often the seat was covered with strips of rawhide crisscrossed in a basketry weave. In many of the present Spanish homes this bench is covered with white bleached rawhide. The large armchairs of similar design also have rawhide seats. Benches that are to be used on the patio often have the rawhide stretched over them with the hair left on.

CONSTRUCTION

This plate and illustration show most of the details of construction. The tenon on the front rail is offset to miss the through tenon from the end rail. If the rawhide seat is used, a similar rail must be placed between the back legs to support the weaving, and the structure should be braced with heavy cornerpieces. The wood seat should be notched to fit the legs, and should be secured with screws. Holes should be counterbored to a depth of ½ inch for the heads. The seat must be in position before the arms are fastened on. The shape of the arms is arbitrary, since a great variety of shapes were used by the early Spanish craftsmen.

CARVING AND DESIGN

The offset design on the back as well as that on the tops of the back legs is characteristic of the earlier pieces. Details of the crosspieces are shown in the plate.

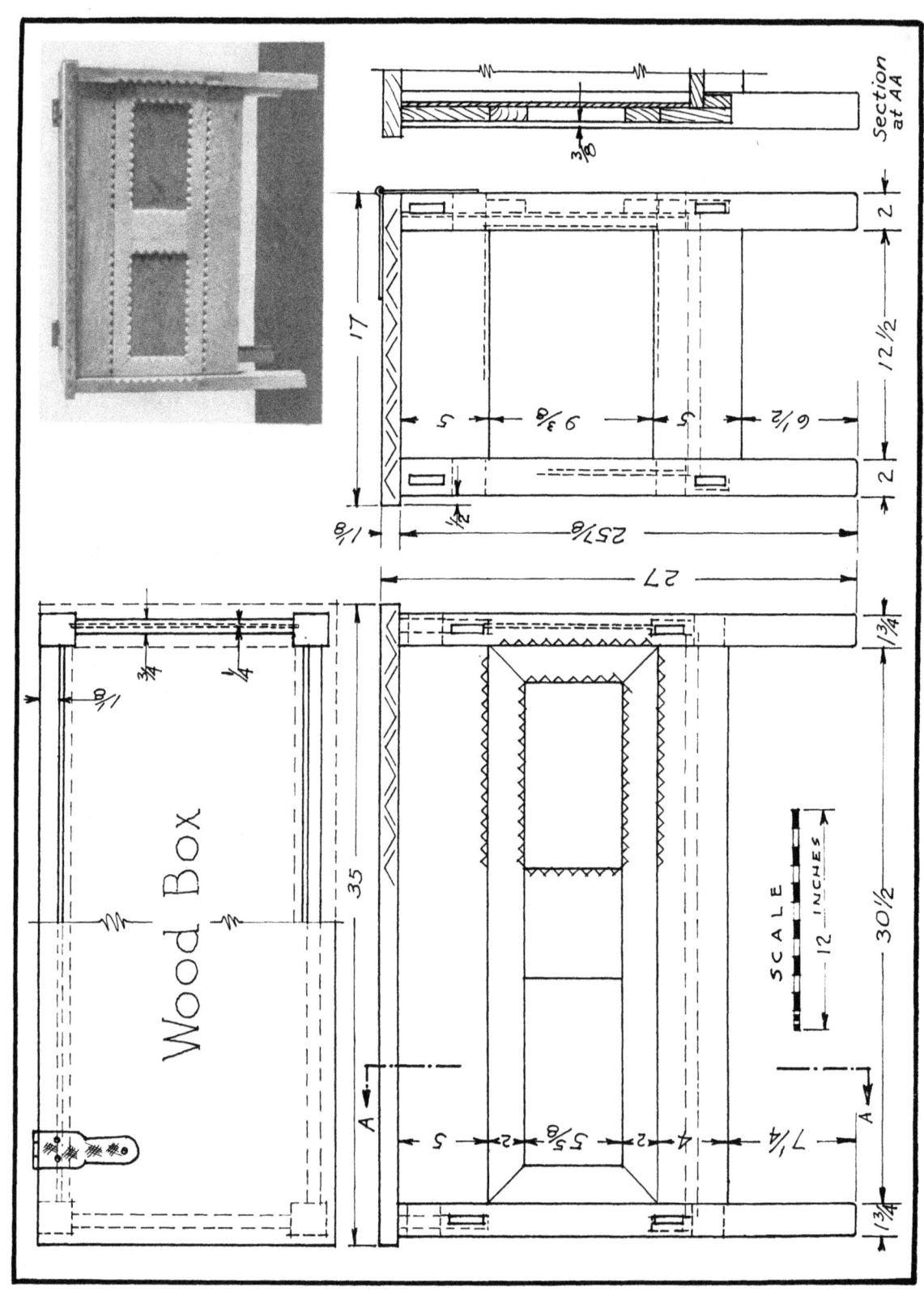

Wood Box

BILL OF MATERIAL

Pieces

4	1¾ by 2 by 25⅞	Legs
4	¾ by 5 by 16½	End rails
2	¼ by 9⅞ by 13	End panels
2	¾ by 4 by 34	Bottom rails
1	¾ by 5 by 34	Top rail (front)
1	1⅛ by 5 by 34	Top rail (back)
4	¾ by 2 by 30½	Rails for front and back panels
4	¾ by 2 by 9⅝	Rails for front and back panels
2	¾ by 6 by 6⅝	Centerpieces for front and back panels
2	¼ by 16 by 30½	Ply for panels
4	3/16 by 2½ by 8¾	Metal hinges
2	¾ by 1½ by 30½	Bottom supports
2	¾ by 2¼ by 12½	Bottom supports
1	¾ by 14 by 33	Bottom
1	1⅛ by 17 by 35	Top

The wood box was a necessary article of furniture in every colonial household. It was found in the living room as well as in the kitchen. In fact, it was found wherever there was a fireplace, and this was sometimes in every room of the house. Only the kindling and dry wood were kept in this box; the heavier logs were elsewhere. The top had to be strong enough so that it could be used as a bench or love seat. The wood box stands by the fireplace today, a reminder of colonial romance.

CONSTRUCTION

The crosspieces on the sides and ends are all the same width and are fastened with through mortise-and-tenon joints. The tenons are offset from the centers so they will not cross each other at the corners. All the pieces except the front are grooved to take the panels. The panels in the front are set to take the frames before being fastened in place with dowel rods. The hinges are hammered and decorated as shown in the top view of the box. They should be fastened on with decorative rivets. These hinges can be shaped from regular strap hinges, hammered and treated with acid.

CARVING

A meander design is developed on the edges by taking out triangular chips on alternate sides. The rest of the carving is a series of chips taken at regular intervals. It certainly is not very difficult carving. It is referred to in the shop as jackknife carving, but it is quite characteristic of the Spanish colonial period.

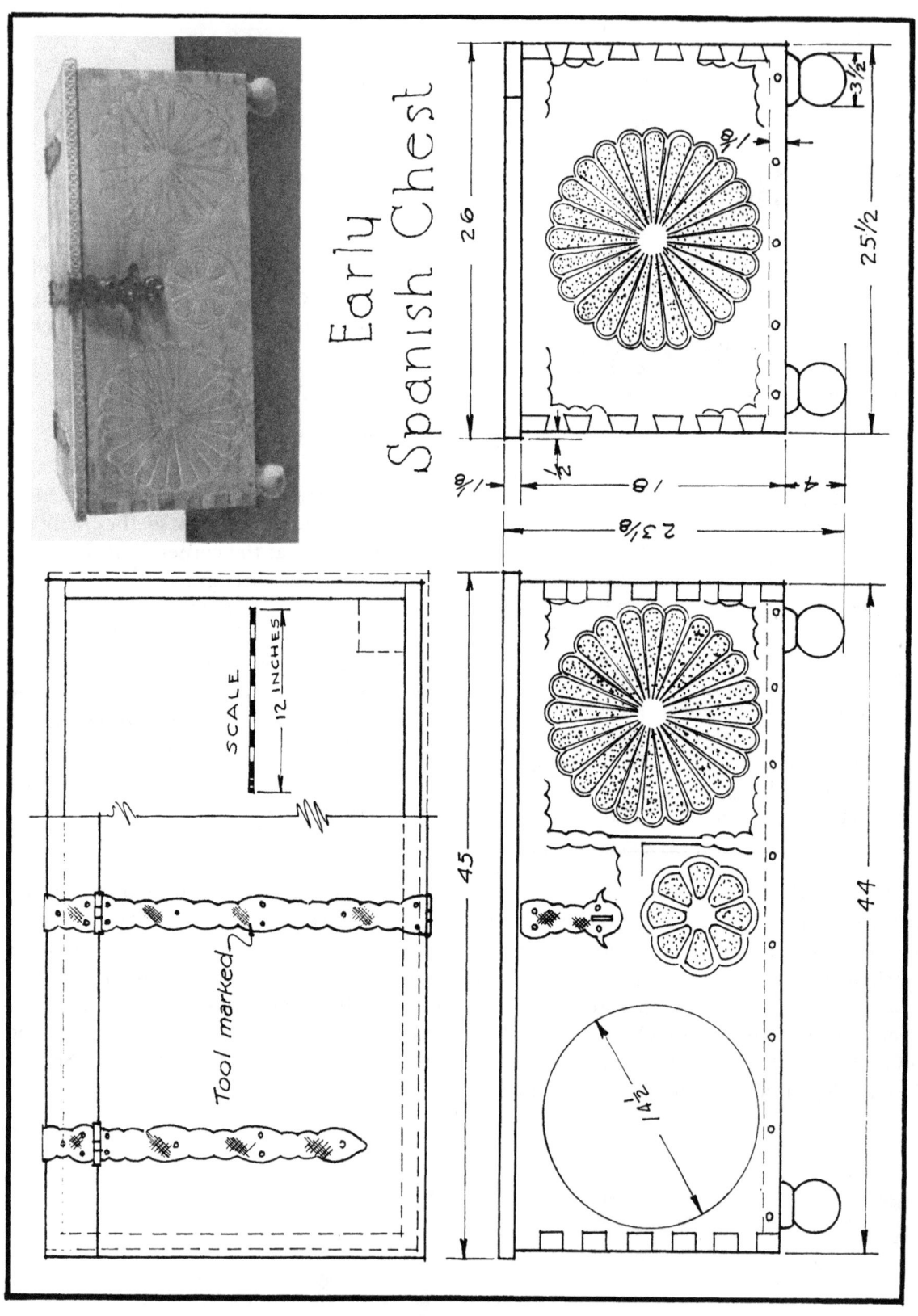

Early Spanish Chest

Early Spanish Chest

BILL OF MATERIAL
Pieces
4	3½ by 3½ by 5⅛	Feet
2	1⅛ by 18 by 44	Sides
2	1⅛ by 18 by 25½	Ends
1	1⅛ by 24¼ by 41¾	Bottom
1	1⅛ by 26 by 45	Top
1	3/16 by 2 by 72	Strap-iron hinges

This chest is to a large extent a reproduction of an antique. The designs are hammered into the wood with a blunt instrument. The wrought-iron hinges and the hasp are copied, and the padlock was produced in the blacksmith shop. The feet are the same as those in the original. The carving on the edge of the lid was taken from the Spanish.

CONSTRUCTION

The corners are dovetailed and pinned from top and bottom. They need no reinforcement and will last. The sides and ends are grooved to take the bottom, which is held in place by ⅜-inch dowel rods. The feet are mortised through the bottom and are wedged on the inside. The wedges are made at right angles to the grain of the wood. They are shaped out of 4 by 4-inch stock by hand. The top is two pieces. It extends over the ends and front ½ inch. The three hinges are fastened in place by decorative rivets. The center hinge and hasp extend across the entire top; the other two hinges extend to within 3 inches of the front edge. Details of these are shown in the top view.

CARVING

The figures are outlined by light carving, about ⅛-inch deep. The different elements of the design are hammered with a blunt instrument such as a heavy center punch. The weight of the instrument is sufficient to make the design. Each end is similar to one large completed design on the front. There is no carving on the top. Details of the chip carving suggested for the edge of the top are shown in the special chapter.

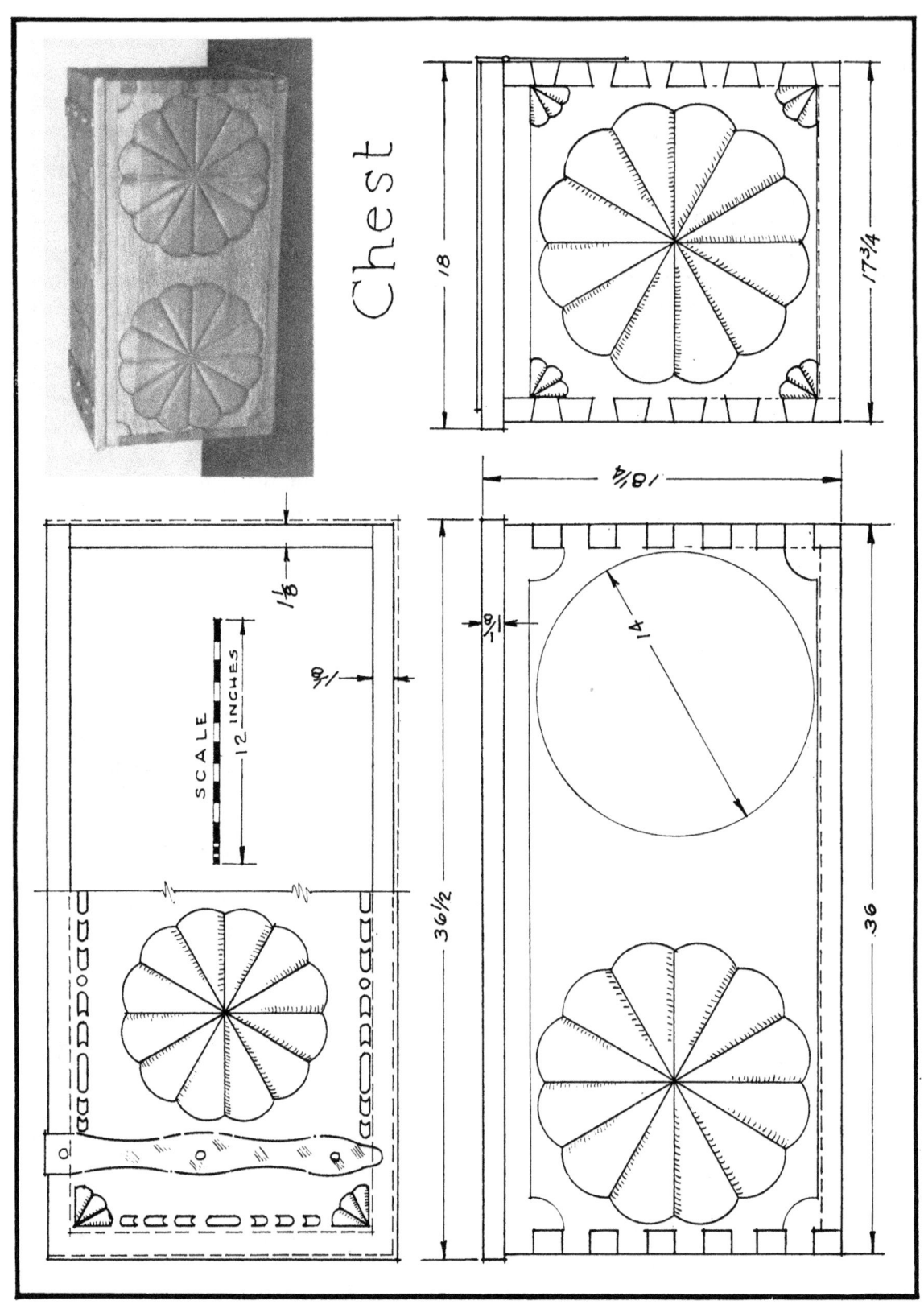

Chest

BILL OF MATERIAL

Pieces			
2	1⅛ by 17⅛ by 17¾	Ends
2	1⅛ by 17⅛ by 36	Sides
1	1⅛ by 16¾ by 35	Bottom
1	1⅛ by 18 by 36½	Top
2	3/16 by 2 by 24	Metal for hinges

A chest was a necessary furnishing of the early Spanish colonial home. A grain box, as well as a wood box, usually was found in the kitchen. These boxes had drop lids, ornamental hinges, and quite often handmade locks. When used in the living room, the chest was mounted on legs; the front side would be hinged to drop down on supports that pulled out from beneath, and in this way would serve as a writing desk. The interior then had numerous drawers and pigeonholes. In the bedroom, a chest similar to the one shown was used for storage.

CONSTRUCTION

First, the sides and ends are cut to size. As indicated, the dovetail corners are laid out with a T bevel and a rule. The portions to be cut out are marked on the wood with an O. The ends are cut out first, and the sides are cut to match. Before assembling, the carving is done on the front, top, and two ends. The sides and ends are grooved on the inside, so the bottom will be completely covered by the sides. The joints are glued and assembled with plenty of clamps. The corners are tied into place by ⅜-inch dowel rods on both top and bottom. The bottom is cut to fit and fastened into place with 2-inch, No. 10 screws. The top is made to extend about ¼ inch over the front so it can be lifted readily.

CARVING AND HINGES

The carving consists of six large rosettes on the top, front, and two ends. The border on the top is made with a ½-inch gouge. The designs should be well sanded to bring out the grain of the wood. The hinges are made of 3/16-inch strap iron. They are shaped, hammered, and decorated with imitation heads of rivets. Instead of making the complete hinge, these top pieces can be welded onto 2-inch iron butts. If a lock is used, a third hinge is placed in the center and to this a hasp is attached that falls over the front edge into the lock. Hasp and lock should be handmade.

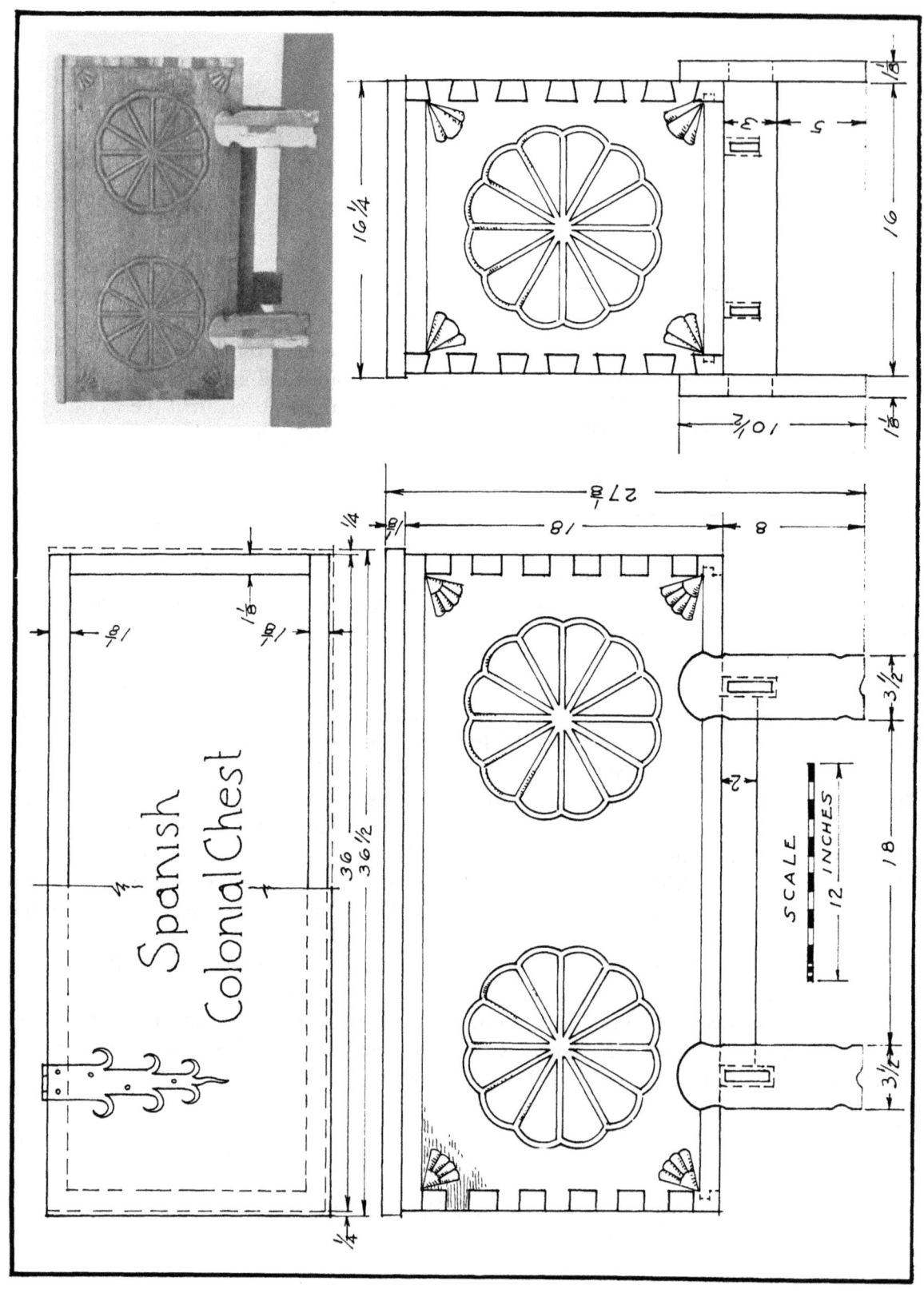

Spanish Colonial Chest

Spanish Colonial Chest

BILL OF MATERIAL

Pieces		
2	1⅛ by 18 by 36	Sides
2	1⅛ by 18 by 16	Ends
1	1⅛ by 16¼ by 36½	Top
1	1⅛ by 15 by 35	Bottom
4	1⅛ by 3½ by 10½	Base uprights
2	1⅛ by 3 by 18¼	Base rests
2	1⅛ by 2 by 23	Base stretchers

The coloring on this chest is exceptional. The front is made of one piece, but the heartwood contrasts strikingly with the sapwood. The base is typically Spanish colonial. The size is convenient; it is easy to move and is low enough to be used as a seat. These chests are suitable for any room of the home, and are sufficiently pretentious to grace a front and entrance hall.

CONSTRUCTION

True dovetail corners are more appropriate than any other method of construction. Carefully fitted dovetails will keep the sides from warping. Dovetail corners are not hard to do if they are laid out accurately. The front and back are laid out first and sawed to the lines. The ends are laid out and checked with the sides before sawing to be sure they are right. All corners are fitted before carving. The full depth of the bottom is grooved to within ½ inch of the outside so the bottom will be flush with the sides and ends. The top extends over the front and ends by about ¼ inch.

CARVING

The large rosettes on the front exhibit the essential characteristics of the early Spanish colonial designs, as do the contours of the base. Each end has a single rosette similar to those on the front. The top is the same as the front with the exception that the rosettes are smaller to leave a flat surface for the hinges. The wrought-iron hinges should extend well across the top. They are cut from 3/16 by 2½-inch stock and are ornamented with rivets having oval heads. If these rivet heads are made from ½ to ¾ inch in diameter, they will add to the attractiveness of the piece.

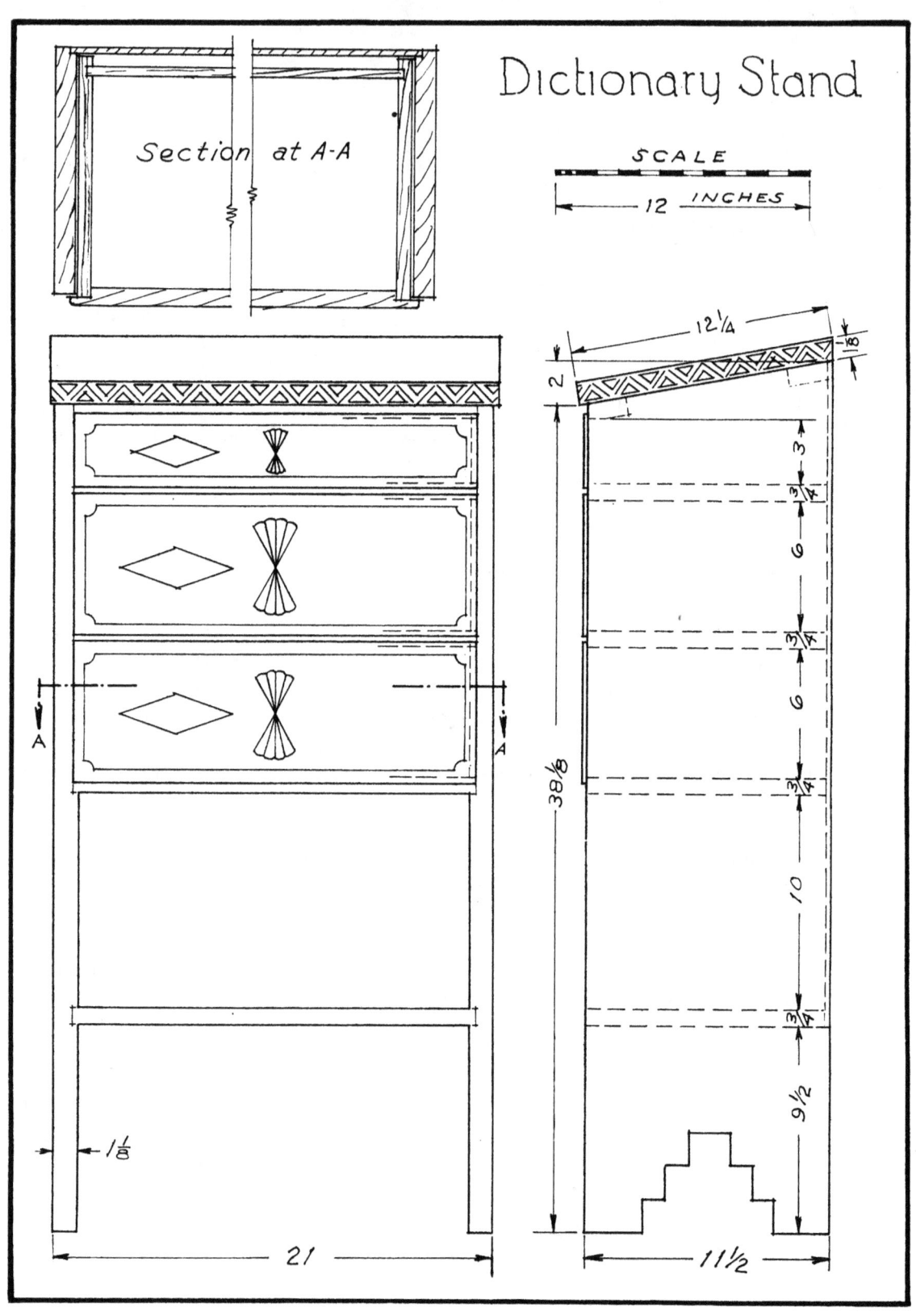

Dictionary Stand

BILL OF MATERIAL

Pieces

2	1⅛ by 11½ by 40⅛	Ends
1	¾ by 11¼ by 19¾	Shelf
3	¾ by 11¼ by 19¾	Frames, drawer supports
2	¾ by 2 by 19¾	Top stretchers
1	1⅛ by 12¼ by 22	Top
1	¼ by 19¾ by 30⅝	Back
2	¾ by 6½ by 19¾	Drawer fronts
1	¾ by 3½ by 19¾	Drawer front
4	¾ by 6 by 11	Drawer sides
2	¾ by 3 by 11	Drawer sides
2	¾ by 5¼ by 17¾	Drawer backs
1	¾ by 2¼ by 17¾	Drawer back
3	¼ by 11 by 17¾	Drawer bottoms

One would think that ordinarily a dictionary stand would have no place in the furnishing of a Spanish home, but it can be used to advantage in the study or den. The present piece was originally designed for a schoolroom, in which the tables, chairs, and desks were Spanish. The bottom shelf can be used for books or a typewriter.

CONSTRUCTION

There are no difficult problems of construction, yet it offers a variety of interesting operations for the craftsman and student. The two ends are cut to the desired size, with the back 2 inches longer than the front. Grooves ½ inch deep are sawed to take the shelf and drawer supports. Three frames for drawer supports are made the same size as the shelf, which is ¼ inch less in width than the ends. The tops of the ends are grooved on the inside to take ¾ by 2-inch tie pieces. The parts are glued up, tested for squareness, and the tie pieces are nailed in place. The top extends ½ inch over the front and ends. The drawer fronts extend over the openings by ¼ inch at top and bottom, and ½ inch at each end.

CARVING AND DESIGN

The double fan-shaped design in the center of the drawer fronts is adapted from the early colonial. The diamond-shaped depressions where the drawer pulls are located are cut to a depth of about ⅛ inch. The outer quadrilateral is outlined by depressions cut with a ¼-inch gouge. These are the so-called bullet designs. The rest of the outlined portion is cut away, leaving the border about 3/16 inch in relief. This portion is smoothed with a broad, sharp chisel and sanded. The edge is the No. 4 pattern described on page 13.

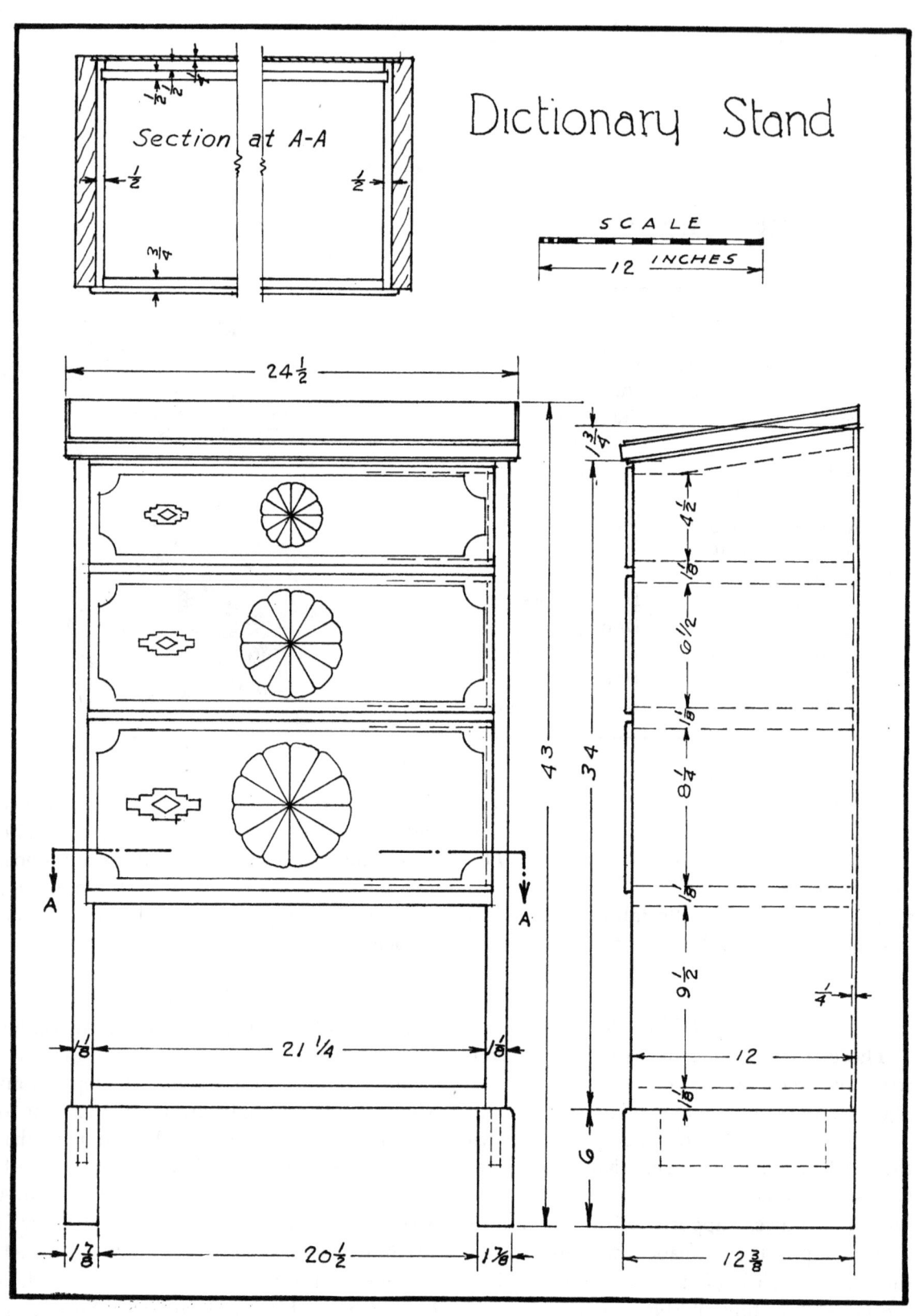

Dictionary Stand

BILL OF MATERIAL

Pieces

2	1⅞ by 6 by 12⅜	Base
2	1⅛ by 12 by 38⅜	Ends
1	1⅛ by 11¾ by 21¼	Shelf
4	1⅛ by 11¾ by 22¼	Drawer-support frames
1	1⅛ by 13 by 24½	Top
1	¾ by 9¼ by 22¼	Drawer front
1	¾ by 7½ by 22¼	Drawer front
1	¾ by 5½ by 22¼	Drawer front
2	½ by 8¼ by 11¾	Drawer sides
2	½ by 6½ by 11¾	Drawer sides
2	½ by 4½ by 11¾	Drawer sides
1	½ by 7½ by 20¾	Drawer back
1	½ by 5¾ by 20¾	Drawer back
1	½ by 3¾ by 20¾	Drawer back
3	¼ by 11¾ by 20¾	Drawer bottoms
1	¼ by 21¾ by 35¾	Back

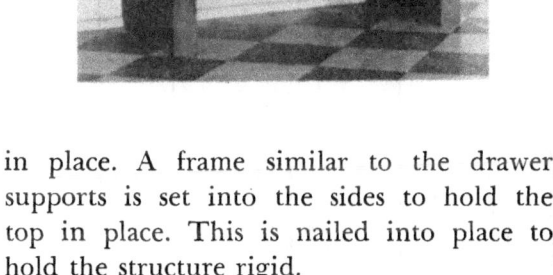

This dictionary stand was designed and made for the author's office. It has proved to be a useful piece and has been admired by all who have seen it. It can be used to advantage in the home library as well as in the schoolroom.

CONSTRUCTION

The sides are cut to the indicated size and dadoes are cut to take the drawer supports. A 3-inch long tenon holds them securely to the base. The shelf ties the bottom together. The drawer supports are 1⅛-inch stock, securely nailed together before being glued in place. A frame similar to the drawer supports is set into the sides to hold the top in place. This is nailed into place to hold the structure rigid.

CARVING

The small designs where the drop pulls are located are of Indian origin. The elements of the rosette are well rounded and polished to show the grain of the wood to advantage. The edges of the top are rounded. They could be carved. The base could be constructed similar to that of the Spanish highboy, or the sides could set directly upon the floor.

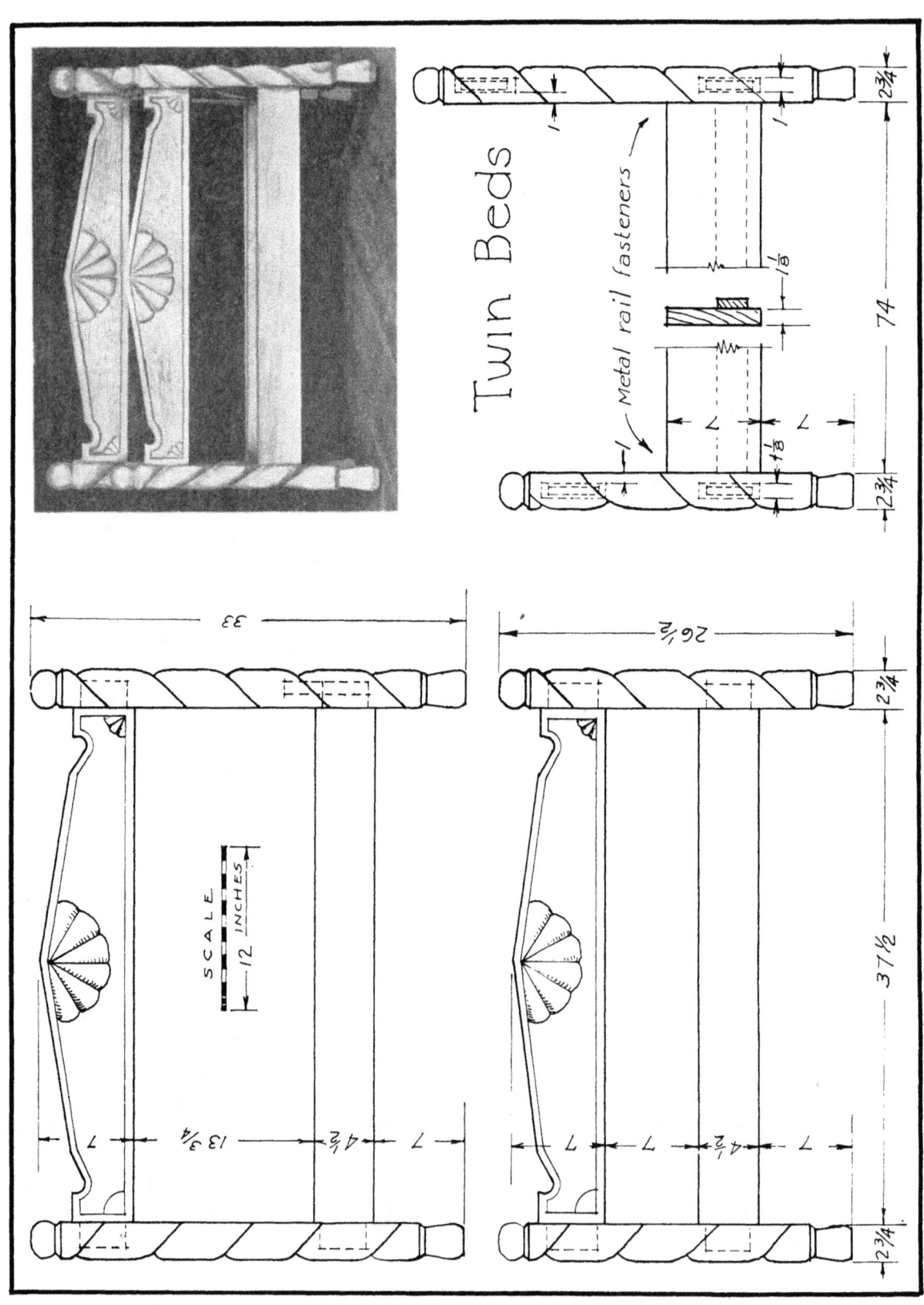

Twin Beds

BILL OF MATERIAL

Pieces

2	2¾ by 2¾ by 33	Headposts
2	2¾ by 2¾ by 26½	Foot posts
2	1⅛ by 7 by 41	Head and foot upper rails
2	1⅛ by 4½ by 41	Head and foot lower rails
2	1⅛ by 7 by 74	Side rails
2	¾ by 2 by 72	Side rail supports
1	Set of bed hardware	

This bed is more popular than the double bed although the latter is more characteristic of the early Spanish colonial. The width of the headpiece should be about the same as that of the foot piece. The heavy inner-spring mattress will cover part of the footboard so the carving should be limited to the outside of the foot. Since the head is generally set against a wall the carving should be done on the inside or front only.

CONSTRUCTION

The tenons on the crosspieces are made as long as possible, to make a solid head and foot. Regular bed hardware is used for the side rails. The width should vary to fit the box springs, so that supports can be fastened to the insides of the rails. Beds vary in width, so the dimensions are arbitrary.

CARVING

The spirals are carved on only two sides of the legs until the construction is finished; then all exposed parts are carved. The head and footpieces are carved before putting them together. The knobs are round but could be elongated. The chisel marks are not sanded out on the knobs, but the partial rosettes are well rounded and sanded to bring out the grain of the wood.

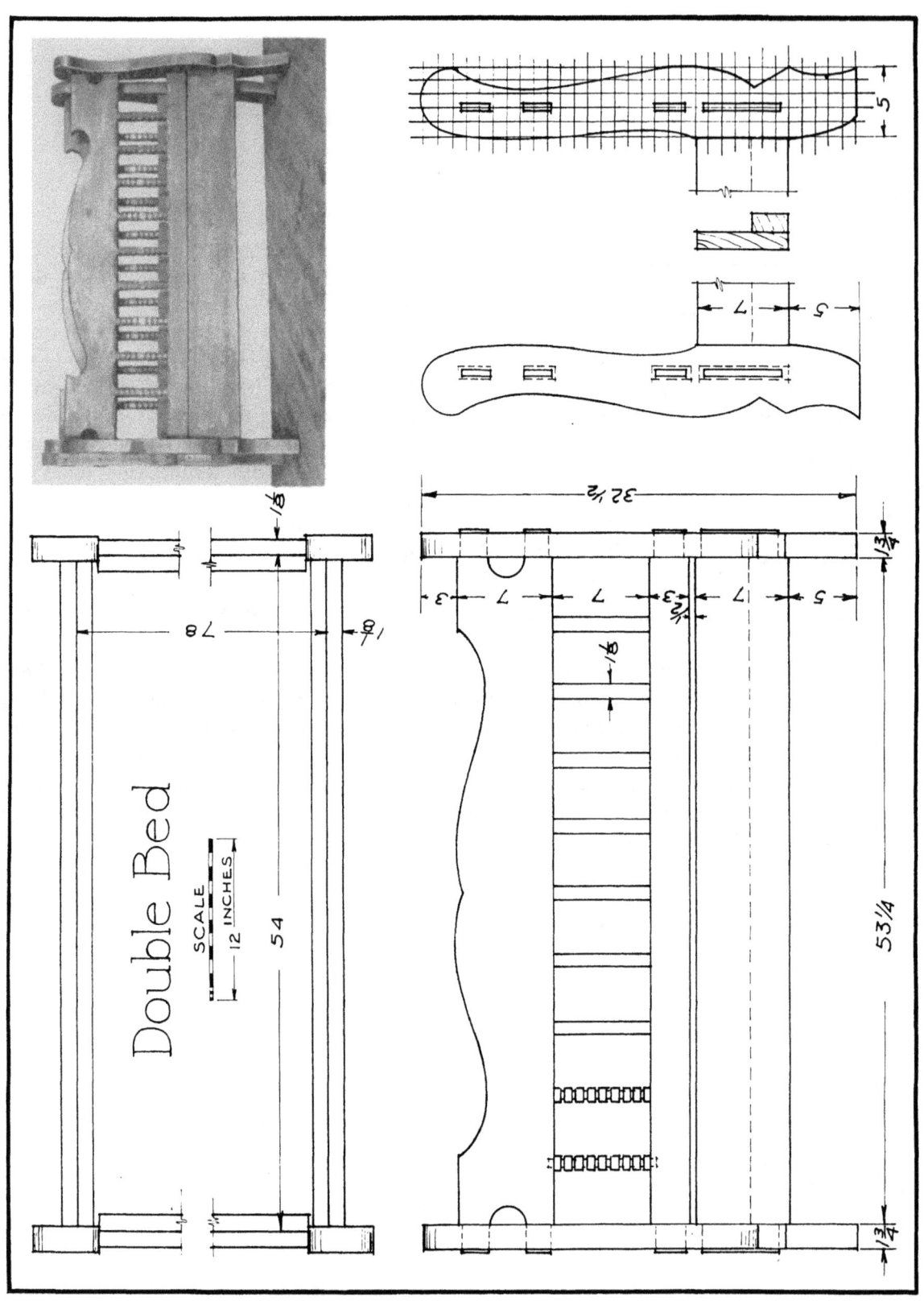

Double Bed

BILL OF MATERIAL

Pieces		
4	1¾ by 5 by 32½	Legs
4	1⅛ by 7 by 57¼	Top and bottom rails, head and foot
2	1⅛ by 3 by 57¼	Center rails, head and foot
18	1⅛ by 1⅛ by 8	Fretwork
2	1⅛ by 7 by 75	Side rails
2	1⅛ by 2¾ by 75	Spring supports, sides
2	1⅛ by 2¾ by 53¼	Spring supports, head and foot

This is a characteristic Spanish colonial bed. The legs are made heavy and solid, and the rounds are left rough. In the old colonial beds, the headpiece and footpiece were quite often painted and decorated with flowers. In making a bed for modern use, it is best to use the same finish that is recommended for the other pieces.

CONSTRUCTION

The head and foot are both the same. Through mortise-and-tenon joints are used in all construction. The tenons extend through about ¼ inch and are beveled. The rounds are turned on the lathe but are left rough, and are mortised about ½ inch into the crosspieces. They are made of 1⅛-inch stock; so the tenons may be made ⅝ inch square. Enough of the surface is left so the tenons can be cut after the turning is done. In the old beds the side rails had on each end a long tenon that fit into mortises in the legs. The tenon was held in place by a pin with a knob on the end for pulling out. This was rather weak, and both the pin and the hole would wear so the bed soon became unsteady. It is best to use regulation hardware throughout the piece.

CARVING

There is very little carving on this bed. After the rounds are turned on the lathe and are fastened in position, they are shaped by hand. The edges between the rounds are beveled. The flat surfaces on the outsides of the legs can be broken up by a carved design. The shape of the headpiece can be varied to suit the individual taste.

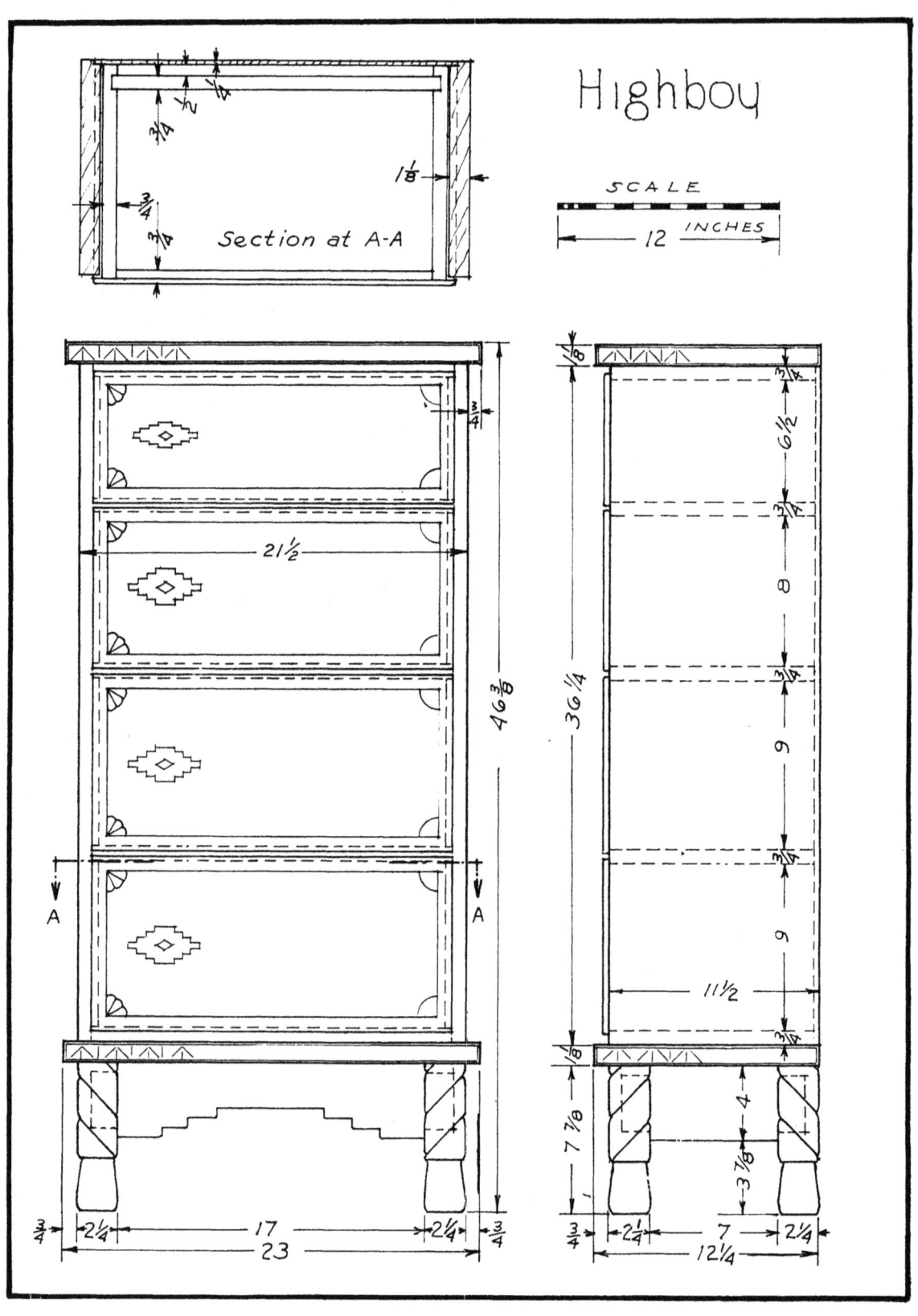

Highboy

BILL OF MATERIAL

Pieces

BOTTOM SECTION

4	2¼ by 2¼ by 7⅞	Legs
2	1⅛ by 4 by 20	Front and back rails
2	1⅛ by 4 by 10	End rails
1	1⅛ by 12¼ by 23	Top

TOP SECTION

2	1⅛ by 11½ by 36¼	Ends
2	¾ by 9½ by 20	Drawer fronts
1	¾ by 8½ by 20	Drawer front
1	¾ by 7 by 20	Drawer front
4	¾ by 9 by 11	Drawer ends
2	¾ by 8 by 11	Drawer ends
2	¾ by 6½ by 11	Drawer ends
2	¾ by 8¼ by 18	Drawer backs
1	¾ by 7¼ by 18	Drawer back
1	¾ by 5¾ by 18	Drawer back
4	¼ by 11 by 18	Drawer bottoms
1	¼ by 20 by 36¼	Back
1	1⅛ by 12¼ by 23	Top
5	Frames for drawer supports; outside dimensions, ¾ by 11¼ by 20	

This high, narrow chest of drawers was made to fit a wall space between two doors. It is not very deep, but it does afford much drawer space, and is a handy piece of furniture to hold small articles that the homeowner wants to keep in a readily accessible place. It is substantial and heavy, but does not have a massive appearance. It will harmonize with the other articles of furniture found in a Spanish type of home.

CONSTRUCTION

The base is built as a unit, with the top the same size as the top of the chest. The top of this unit can be made of low-grade material just so the edge is clear of knots for carving. It can be fastened onto the rails with screws, as the heads will be covered with the top unit. The ends of the top unit are cut to the sizes indicated, and grooves are cut with the dado head to take the drawer supports. Five frames of uniform size are made, well nailed together from the ends. The three middle ones are glued into place and the other two are nailed from the top and bottom. This unit is fastened to the base by screws through the bottom drawer support, and the top is secured in a similar fashion. The frames for the drawer supports should be ¼ inch less than the width of the ends, so the back panel will be flush. The ends also should be grooved to take the panel.

CARVING AND DESIGN

The legs are carved on two sides only, the ridge of the spiral running from each corner. The chip carving of the edges is the conventional design described in the special chapter on carving. The drawer fronts have a three-unit rosette in each corner. The step-up design varies in size with the size of the drawer. It is left in relief by carving away with a ¼-inch gouge. The drop pulls are regulation size as described elsewhere.

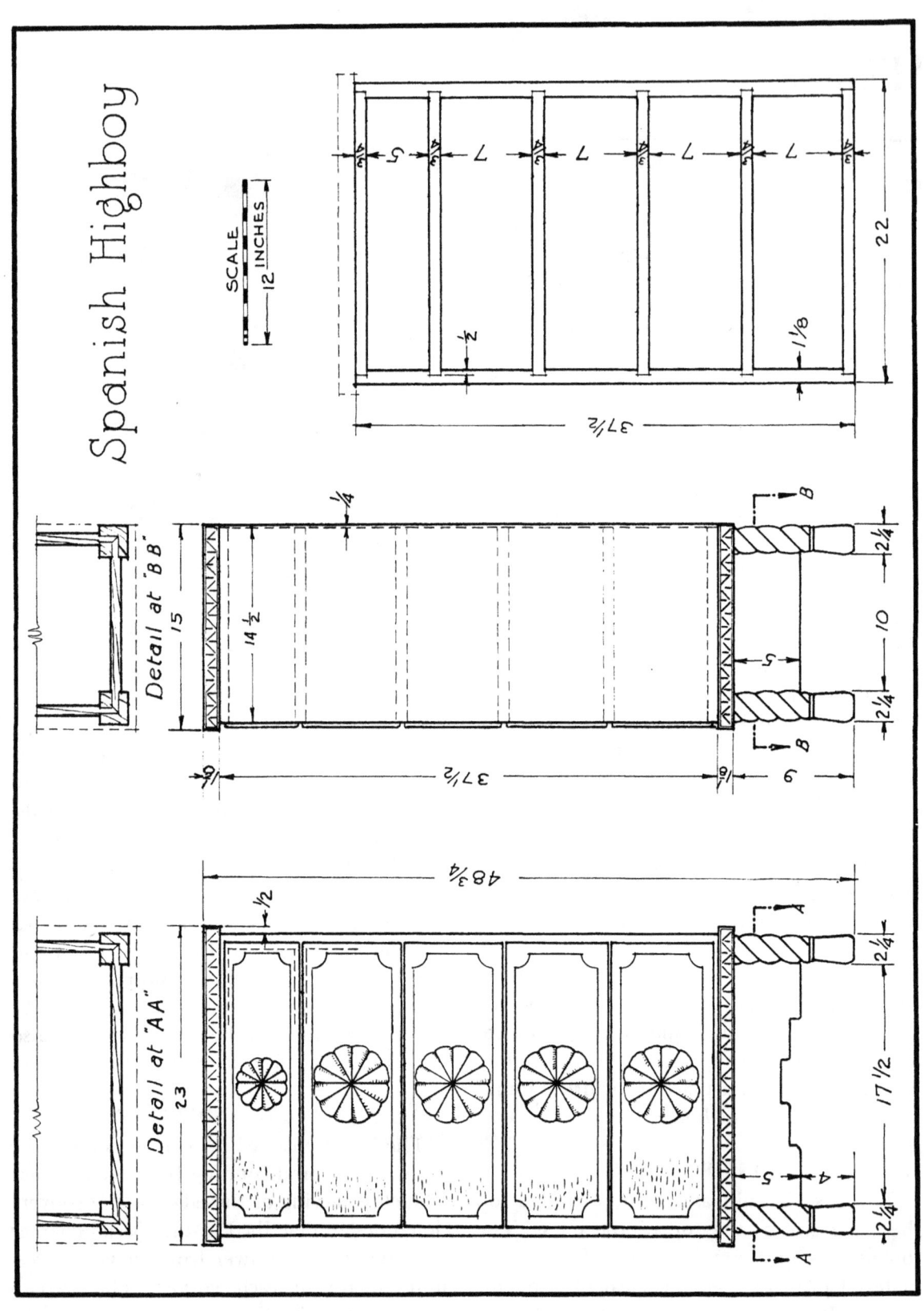

Spanish Highboy

BILL OF MATERIAL

Pieces

4	2¼ by 2¼ by 9	Legs
2	1⅛ by 5 by 20½	Front and back rails of lower unit
2	1⅛ by 5 by 13	Side rails of lower unit
2	1⅛ by 15 by 23	Tops of upper and lower units
2	1⅛ by 14½ by 37½	End pieces of top unit
6	¾ by 14¼ by 20¾	Drawer supports
1	¼ by 20¼ by 37½	Back

SMALL DRAWER

1	1⅛ by 5¾ by 20½	Drawer front
2	½ by 5 by 13¾	Drawer sides
1	½ by 4¼ by 18¾	Drawer back
1	¼ by 14 by 18¾	Drawer bottom

4 LARGE DRAWERS

4	1⅛ by 7¾ by 20½	Drawer fronts
8	½ by 7 by 13¾	Drawer sides
4	½ by 6¼ by 18¾	Drawer backs
4	¼ by 14 by 18¾	Drawer bottoms

The highboy is a very convenient article of furniture for a small room. It doesn't crowd the room, but gives an atmosphere of spaciousness and repose. It is well proportioned, the lines are conservative, and the elements of design are simple. Although designed for a bedroom, this particular piece may stand beside the door in a living room and serve a useful purpose.

CONSTRUCTION

The base is built as a unit. The construction is similar to that for the low chest of drawers. (See p. 109.) The two endpieces for the top unit are cut to size, grooved to take the drawer supports and also at top and bottom to take the ¾ by 3-inch crosspieces. Some material can be saved by using frames instead of solid pieces for the drawer supports. Frames for these drawer supports are built of ¾ by 2¾-inch stock running the long way and ¾ by 1¼ inches the short way, and are nailed from the ends. These frames are built to set ¼ inch in from the back to take the back panel. The sides are also grooved ¼ inch to take the back panel. This top unit is fastened to the bottom with 1½-inch No. 10 flathead screws. The top is fastened in a similar manner from beneath. No nails or screws show.

CARVING

The legs, which are carved on two sides only, should be large enough to look substantial. The rosette should vary with the size of the drawer, and should not be too large so as to crowd the space. The particular type of edge carving shown on the top and bottom looks well, but can be varied to suit individual taste. The edge carving should carry across the two ends, but no other carving should appear there.

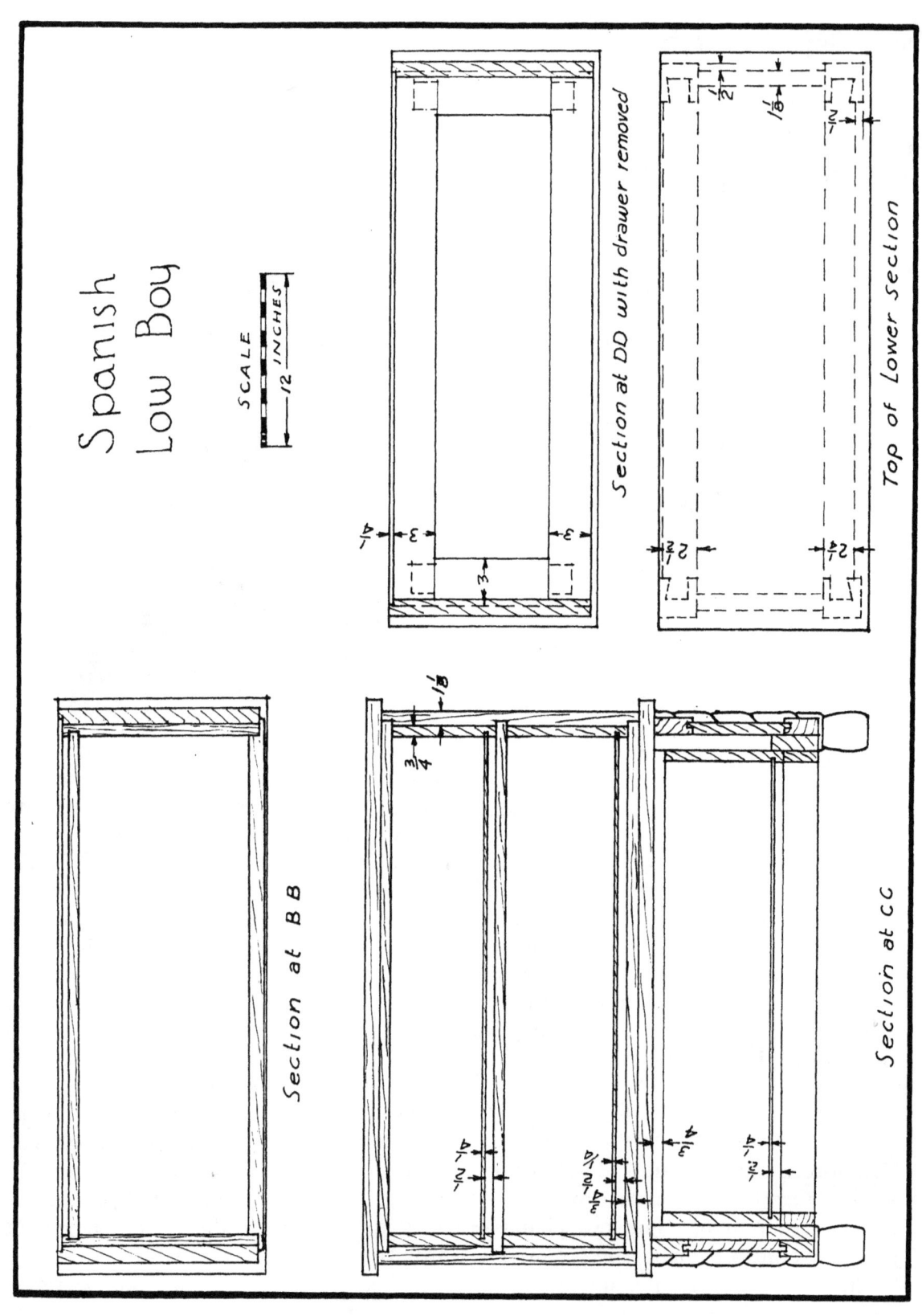

Spanish Lowboy

BILL OF MATERIAL

Pieces

BOTTOM SECTION

4	2¾ by 2¾ by 15¼	Legs
1	¾ by 2¼ by 35½	Top stretcher
1	¾ by 2½ by 35½	Top stretcher
2	¾ by 2½ by 35½	Side rails
2	1⅛ by 2½ by 12½	End rails (lower)
2	1⅛ by 2¾ by 12½	End rails (upper)
2	¾ by 7½ by 10	End panels
1	1⅛ by 15 by 40	Top
1	¼ by 11¾ by 33	Back
2	1⅛ by 3¼ by 9	Drawer guides
2	¾ by 2½ by 12¼	Drawer guides
1	1⅛ by 9¼ by 33	Drawer front
2	¾ by 8½ by 13¾	Drawer sides
1	¾ by 7¾ by 32¼	Drawer back
1	¼ by 13¾ by 32¼	Drawer bottom

TOP SECTION

2	1⅛ by 14½ by 18½	Ends
6	¾ by 3 by 37¼	Rails for drawer support frames
6	¾ by 3 by 12	Rails for drawer support frames
1	¼ by 18½ by 36¾	Back
1	1⅛ by 15 by 40	Top
1	1⅛ by 8 by 37¼	Drawer front
1	1⅛ by 9¼ by 37¼	Drawer front
2	¾ by 8¾ by 14	Drawer sides
2	¾ by 7½ by 14	Drawer sides
1	¾ by 8 by 35½	Drawer back
1	¾ by 6¾ by 35½	Drawer back
2	¼ by 14 by 35½	Drawer bottoms
6	1⅛ by 1⅛ by 3½	Drop pulls

This lowboy was made to special dimensions for a customer. It proved to be an effective and useful piece of furniture, and hence it is being included in this collection. The drawer fronts contained a lot of sap, which gave a beautiful effect to the rosettes. It was made low to fit a space beneath a bedroom window.

CONSTRUCTION

The legs are tied together at the top with dovetail joints and the bottom with mortise-and-tenon joints. They are grooved ½ inch deep to take the end panels which are of ¾-inch stock. The supports for the bottom drawer are notched to fit the legs and are secured with screws to hold the panels in place. The top for the base is held in place by 2-inch screws, the heads of which are covered by the ends of the top section. The ends of the top section are grooved to take the drawer separator and the top and bottom crosspieces. These crosspieces are securely nailed to the ends. This section is fastened to the bottom with screws, and the top is secured to the frame with 1½-inch screws. No nails or screws should show. The bottom drawer end can set inside the legs and flush with the front; the top drawers extend over the opening.

CARVING

The legs are carved on two sides only. The groove starts from each corner and the spiral turns out on each leg, in the front view. Chip carving is used on the edges. The corners of the two top drawers have a decorative scheme. The bottom drawer does not follow the same scheme.

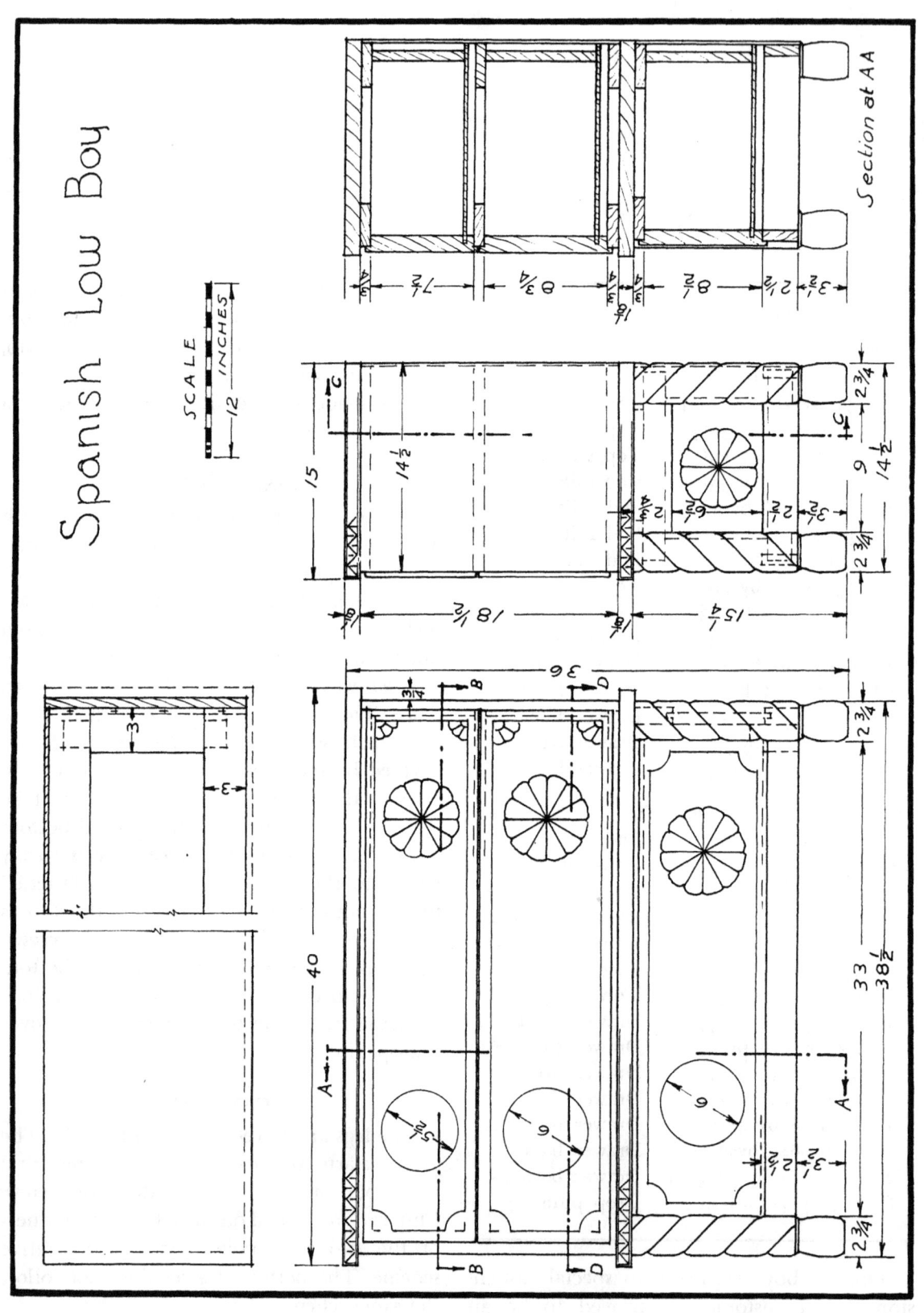

Small Desk

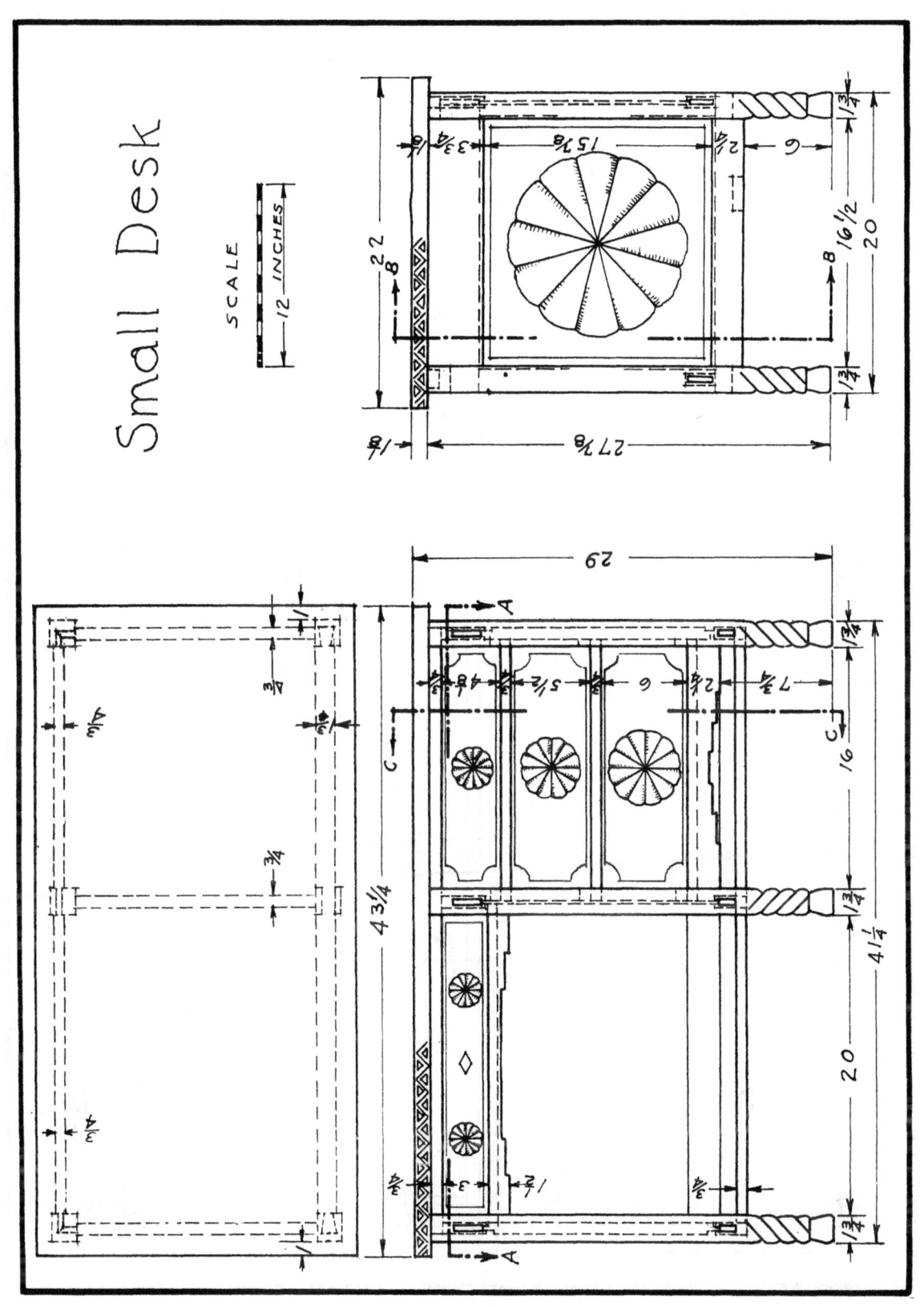

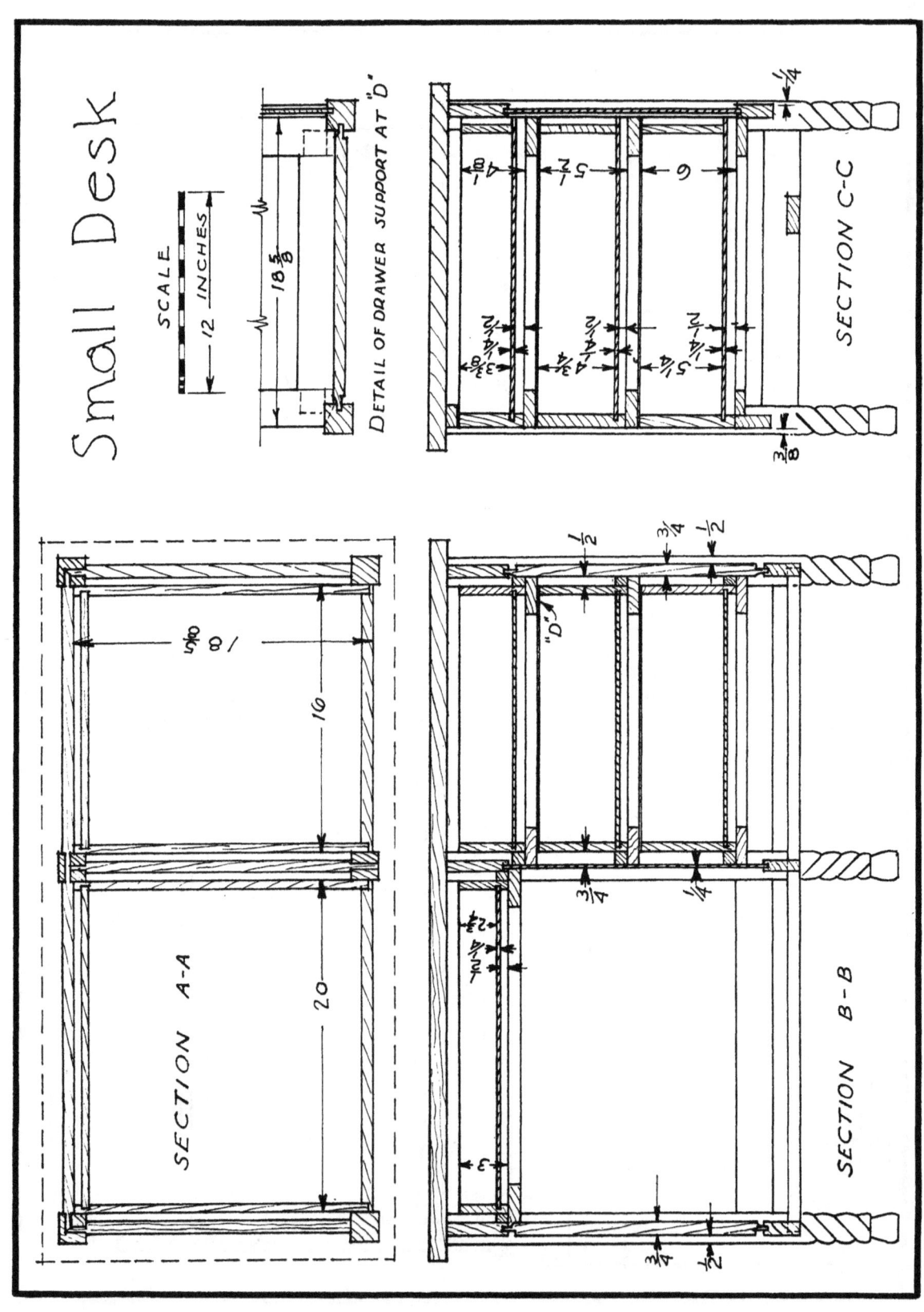

Small Desk

BILL OF MATERIAL

Pieces		
6	1¾ by 1¾ by 27⅞	Legs
3	¾ by 2¼ by 20	Lower rails
3	¾ by 3¾ by 19½	Upper rails
1	¾ by 2¼ by 39¾	Lower back rail
1	¾ by 3¼ by 39¾	Upper back rail
1	¾ by 2¼ by 18	Front apron
1	¾ by 1½ by 22	Front apron
1	¾ by 1⅜ by 39¾	Upper stretcher
2	¾ by 17 by 16⅜	End panels
1	¼ by 17 by 16⅜	Center panel
14	¾ by 2¼ by 17¼	Rails for drawer support frames
2	¾ by 2¼ by 21¼	Rails for drawer support frames
3	¾ by ¾ by 16½	Drawer guides
5	½ by ¾ by 16½	Drawer guides
1	¾ by 2¼ by 39¼	Lower stretcher
1	1⅛ by 22 by 43¼	Top

DRAWERS

1	¾ by 6 by 16	Drawer front
1	¾ by 5½ by 16	Drawer front
1	¾ by 4⅛ by 16	Drawer front
1	¾ by 3 by 20	Drawer front
2	½ by 6 by 18	Drawer sides
2	½ by 5½ by 18	Drawer sides
2	½ by 4⅛ by 18	Drawer sides
2	½ by 3 by 18	Drawer sides
1	½ by 5¼ by 15½	Drawer back
1	½ by 4¾ by 15½	Drawer back
1	½ by 3⅜ by 15½	Drawer back
1	½ by 2¼ by 19½	Drawer back
3	¼ by 15½ by 18	Drawer bottoms
1	¼ by 19½ by 18	Drawer bottom
5	1 by 1 by 3	Drop pulls

There is a great demand for this little desk. Every mother wants to fit up her boy's room with a desk, a high chest of drawers, a bed, and one or two chairs. Such a combination of furniture makes a pleasing environment conducive to study.

The present desk is supplemented with a bench, 16 inches high, that fits under the desk when not in use. The desk is made low enough to accommodate a typewriter. The boy usually wants the top drawer fitted with a lock.

CONSTRUCTION

Through mortise-and-tenon joints are used as a decorative feature and to strengthen the structure. The top is tied together with blind dovetail joints that are set into the top of the two end legs. This stretcher is made wide enough to be notched to fit the center leg, or the leg is notched to fit, as shown in the top view of the plate. The drawer separators are made narrow enough so that the side drawer supports can be notched to fit the legs and nailed in place. However, the construction is largely optional. The bottom stretcher is notched into both ends and the lower crosspiece of the center. It is best to construct the three uprights as units and then tie them together.

CARVING

The end panels are carved from a single piece if possible. The spirals on the legs run close together. The narrow drawer should have two rosettes in order to break up the long, narrow surface. The side carving on the top fits in well with the other designs.

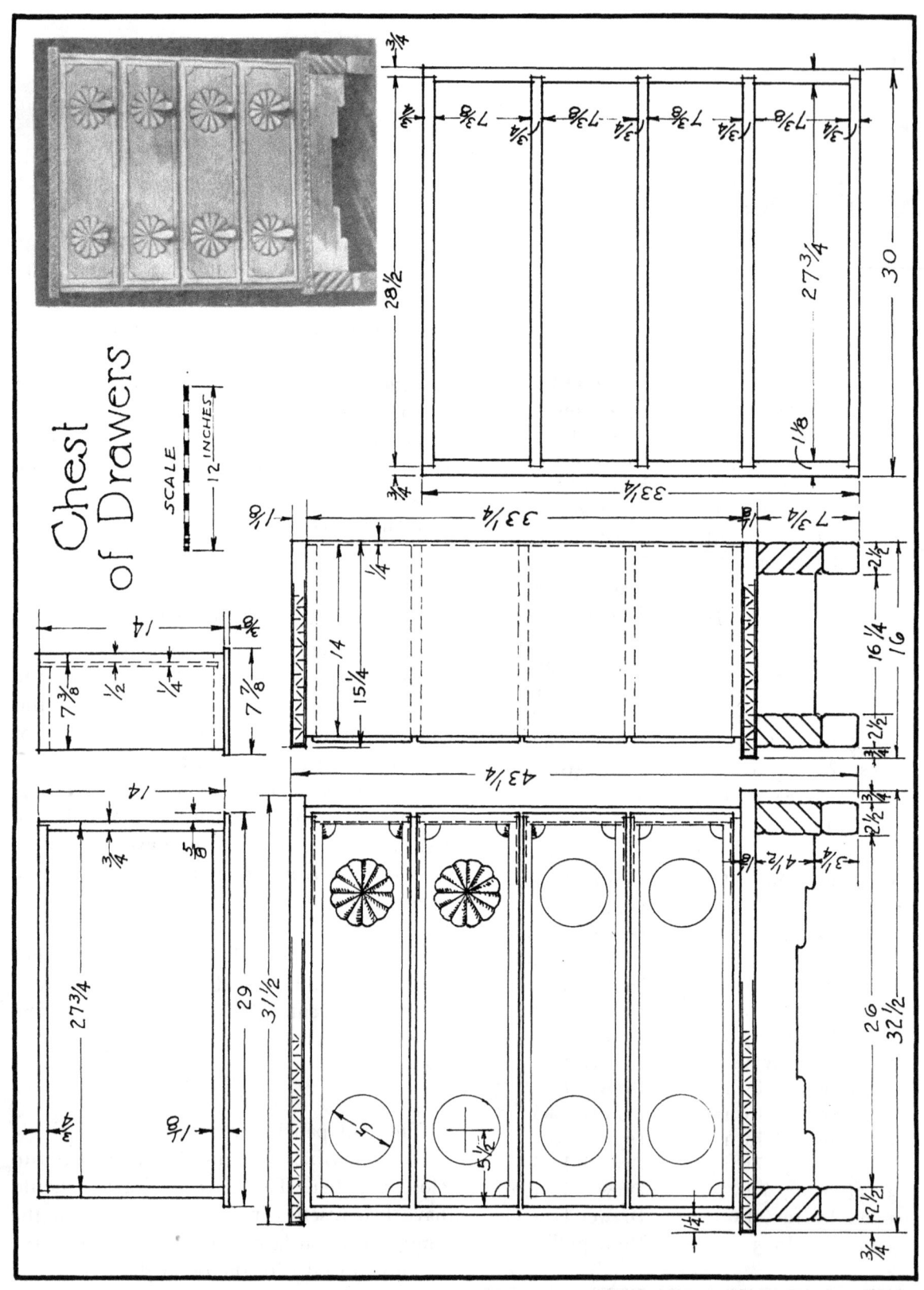

Chest of Drawers

Chest of Drawers

BILL OF MATERIAL

Pieces		
4	$2\frac{1}{2}$ by $2\frac{1}{2}$ by $7\frac{3}{4}$	Legs
2	$1\frac{1}{8}$ by $4\frac{1}{2}$ by 29	Rails
2	$1\frac{1}{8}$ by $4\frac{1}{2}$ by $13\frac{1}{4}$	End rails
2	$1\frac{1}{8}$ by $14\frac{1}{4}$ by $33\frac{1}{4}$	Ends
1	$1\frac{1}{8}$ by $15\frac{1}{4}$ by $31\frac{1}{2}$	Top
1	$1\frac{1}{8}$ by 16 by $32\frac{1}{2}$	Lower top
4	$1\frac{1}{8}$ by $7\frac{7}{8}$ by 29	Drawer fronts
5	$\frac{3}{4}$ by 14 by $28\frac{1}{2}$	Separator frames
1	$\frac{1}{4}$ by $28\frac{1}{4}$ by $33\frac{1}{4}$	Back
8	$\frac{3}{4}$ by $7\frac{3}{8}$ by 14	Drawer sides
4	$\frac{3}{4}$ by $6\frac{5}{8}$ by 27	Drawer backs
4	$\frac{1}{4}$ by $13\frac{5}{8}$ by $26\frac{3}{4}$	Drawer bottoms
8	$1\frac{1}{8}$ by $1\frac{1}{8}$ by $3\frac{1}{2}$	Drawer pulls

A large number of these chests have been made. Some are high and narrow while others are wide and low, depending on the space they are meant to occupy. If the room is small, the narrow chest will fit in best. Most of the chests are conservative in design, following the old patterns as much as possible. The chip carving on the edges has been much in demand. A decorative piece is sometimes used across the back of the top, with the lines on the bottom rail reversed.

CONSTRUCTION

The base is constructed first, using blind mortise-and-tenon joints. The top of the base is similar to the top of the chest, and is fastened to the base by screws through the top which will be covered by the sides. The sides are cut to the desired length and are grooved $\frac{1}{2}$ inch deep and $\frac{3}{4}$ inch wide to take the drawer supports and the crosspieces at top and bottom. The top section is secured to the bottom by screws through these crosspieces. The top is fastened in a similar manner. The sides are grooved $\frac{1}{4}$ inch to take the back panel which is $\frac{1}{4}$-inch plywood. The drawer ends extend $\frac{5}{8}$ inch on each end and $\frac{1}{4}$ inch on top and bottom, making them $1\frac{1}{4}$ inches longer and $\frac{1}{2}$ inch wider than the opening. Frames are made for the drawer supports so that nails are not exposed.

CARVING

The layout for the carving is explained fully in the chapter on carving. The legs are carved on two sides only. The feather outlines on the front rail can be repeated on the ends but not on the back. The feet can be of any shape desired.

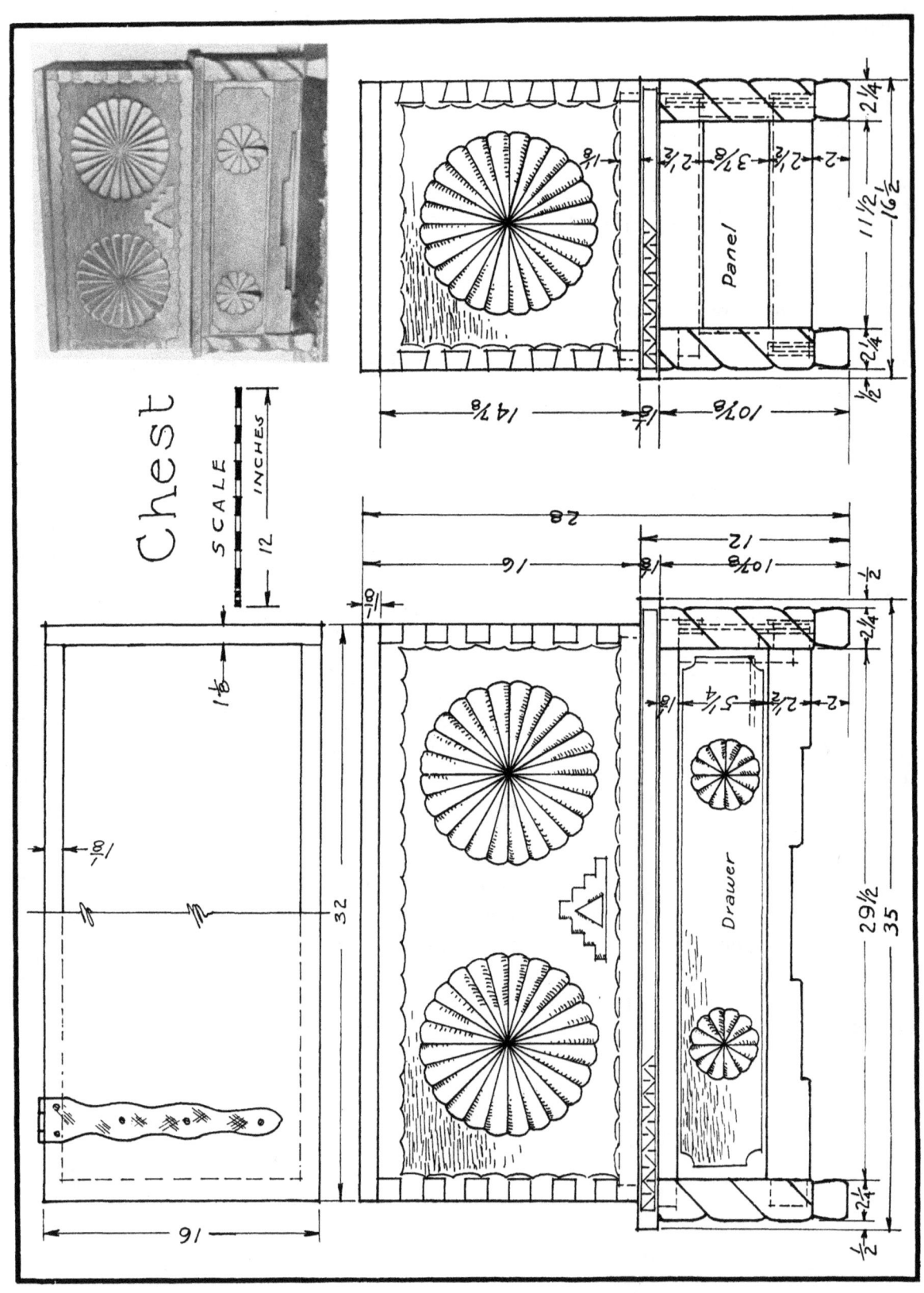

110

Chest

BILL OF MATERIAL

Pieces

LOWER SECTION

4	2¼ by 2¼ by 10⅞	Legs
3	1⅛ by 2½ by 32½	Front and back rails
4	1⅛ by 2½ by 14½	End rails
2	¼ by 4⅜ by 12	End panels
1	¼ by 4⅜ by 30	Back panel
1	1⅛ by 2¼ by 32½	Top stretcher
1	1⅛ by 16½ by 35	Top
1	1⅛ by 5¼ by 29½	Drawer front
2	¾ by 5¼ by 13⅝	Drawer sides
1	¾ by 4½ by 28¾	Drawer back
1	¼ by 13⅞ by 28½	Drawer bottom
2	¾ by 1½ by 12⅝	Drawer supports
2	9/16 by ¾ by 11½	Drawer guides

UPPER SECTION

2	1⅛ by 14⅞ by 32	Front and back
2	1⅛ by 16 by 14⅞	Ends
1	1⅛ by 16 by 32	Top
1	1⅛ by 15 by 31	Bottom
1	Pair of hinges	

A combination chest of this type makes a beautiful piece of furniture for the bedroom. It is well balanced in design and has pleasing proportions. If carefully finished, the carving brings out the beautiful grain of the wood.

CONSTRUCTION

The lower part of the chest is constructed similar to the lower part of the lowboy, and the upper part is constructed similar to the chests described elsewhere in this book. The drop lid should extend over the front slightly so it can easily be lifted.

CARVING

The carving is indicated sufficiently in the plate. The ends of the bottom section often are a solid piece with a large carved rosette. The spiral legs are carved on two sides only. The rosettes on the top section have 24 units, which give a striking contrast with the 12-unit designs of the lower section. The Indian mountain symbol is used on the front. The hinges are very conservative in design. The top can be decorated with two small rosettes and a border design similar to that on the front, or it can be left plain as in the plate.

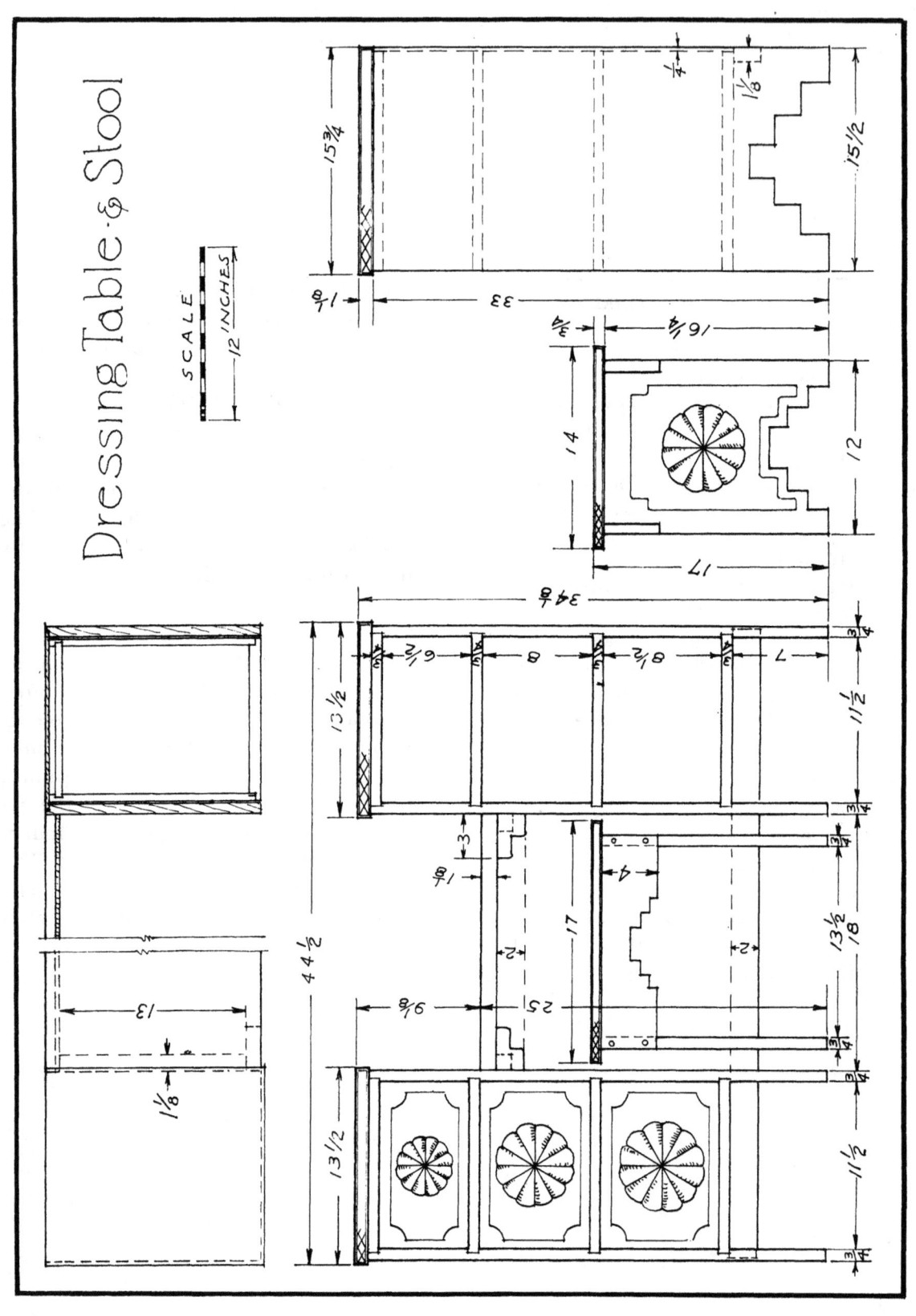

Dressing Table and Stool

BILL OF MATERIAL
Pieces

DRESSING TABLE

4	¾ by 15½ by 33	Ends
8	¾ by 15¼ by 12¼	Drawer supports
2	1⅛ by 13½ by 15¾	Top
2	¼ by 12 by 26	Back
1	¼ by 18 by 18⅞	Back
1	1⅛ by 2 by 18	Upper stretcher
1	1⅛ by 15½ by 18	Shelf
2	1⅛ by 1⅛ by 13	Cleats supporting shelf
2	1⅛ by 2 by 3	Cleats supporting shelf
1	1⅛ by 2 by 43½	Lower stretcher
2	¾ by 8½ by 11½	Drawer fronts
2	¾ by 8 by 11½	Drawer fronts
2	¾ by 6½ by 11½	Drawer fronts
4	¾ by 8½ by 14½	Drawer sides
4	¾ by 8 by 14½	Drawer sides
4	¾ by 6½ by 14½	Drawer sides
2	¾ by 7¾ by 10¾	Drawer backs
2	¾ by 7¼ by 10¾	Drawer backs
2	¾ by 5¾ by 10¾	Drawer backs
6	¼ by 10¾ by 14½	Drawer bottoms

STOOL

2	¾ by 12 by 16¼	Ends
2	¾ by 4 by 15	Apron
1	¾ by 14 by 17	Top

Such a piece of furniture as a dressing table was probably unknown during the Spanish colonial times, yet in the present Spanish home there is a demand for these very types of pieces. This particular table was developed to satisfy a very real need in present-day life.

CONSTRUCTION

Four pieces are cut to the desired size for the ends. They are grooved for the drawer supports and glued up as two units. Frames can be used for drawer supports. The two units are then tied together at the top and bottom by stretchers across the back and braces under the shelf in front.

The bench is made to fit under the table when not in use.

The separate plate mirror hangs on the wall. It could be longer than the one shown here.

CARVING

The carving is rather clearly indicated in the illustration and the plate. However, the two ends of the table were carved with large rosettes. This is optional, depending upon the individual taste of the maker. The piece as it is shown does not seem overdone.

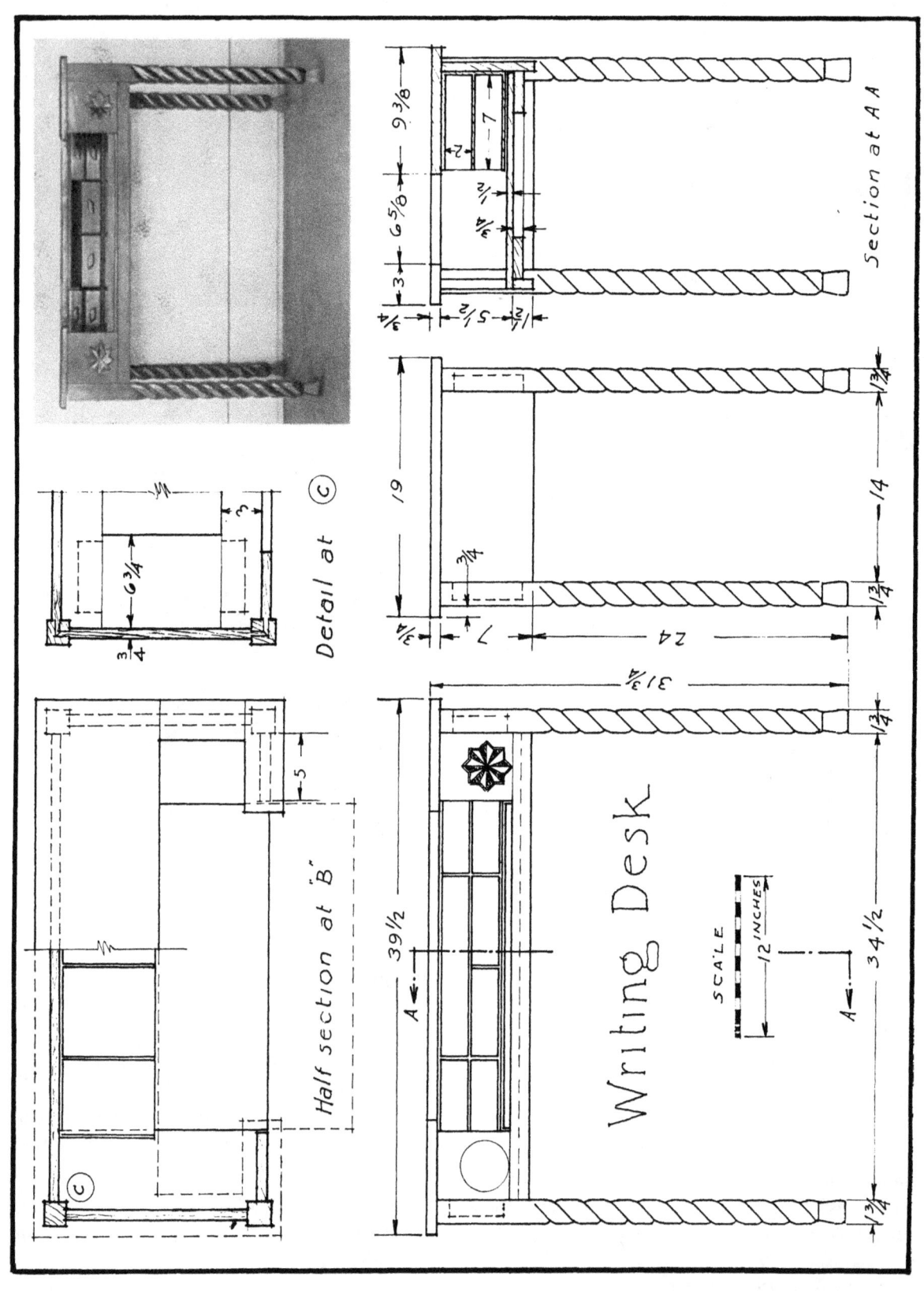

Writing Desk

BILL OF MATERIAL
Pieces

4	1¾ by 1¾ by 31	Legs
1	¾ by 9⅜ by 39½	Top
2	¾ by 3 by 10⅝	Top
2	¾ by 3 by 8½	Top
2	¾ by 7 by 16	End rails
1	¾ by 7 by 36½	Back rail
1	¾ by 1½ by 36½	Front apron
2	¾ by 5½ by 6	Front sections
1	½ by 16 by 24	Writing board
3	⅜ by 7 by 24	Drawer housing
5	¼ by 2⅛ by 7	Drawer separators
2	¾ by 3 by 35½	False bottom
2	¾ by 6¾ by 13	False bottom

Cut stock to fit for drawers

The desk shown here is conservative in lines. It is similar to some of the old Spanish pieces but is not so ornate as were the colonial desks. It can be used in any type of modern home.

CONSTRUCTION

The legs are 29½ inches long, making the top 30½ inches high. This places the writing board at about the right height for a typewriter. The sides and ends are joined to the legs with blind mortise-and-tenon joints, mitered where they meet in the mortise. These are reinforced by flat corner braces. A false bottom of low-grade material is fastened to these braces so that the top of it is even with the cutaway portion of the front rail. The writing board rests upon this and can be pulled out for service. The board should be of 5-ply, ½-inch material. A piece of the same material is inserted at each end of the writing board and is fastened to the false bottom with screws from beneath. The compartments for the drawers, paper, and pigeonholes are built in one section and are fastened to the upper part of the top before the top is secured in place. Top and bottom pieces of this section are of ⅜-inch material and the partitions are ¼ inch. The drawer ends are of ½-inch material, notched to take the sides and bottom. The top is fastened on with desk clips, to allow for contraction. All edges should be well rounded.

CARVING

Very little carving is done on this piece outside of that on the legs. The amount of carving and finish will depend upon the other furniture in the room. The desk illustrated was finished with a dark stain and had very little carving because it was to be used in a room where the other furniture was not Spanish. The drawer pulls are ⅝ by ⅝ by 1¾ inches, and are shaped with a chisel and gouge to the shape indicated in the illustration. The ends are not decorated. If this piece were to be in a room with Spanish colonial furniture, the edges of the top should be decorated as well as the ends.

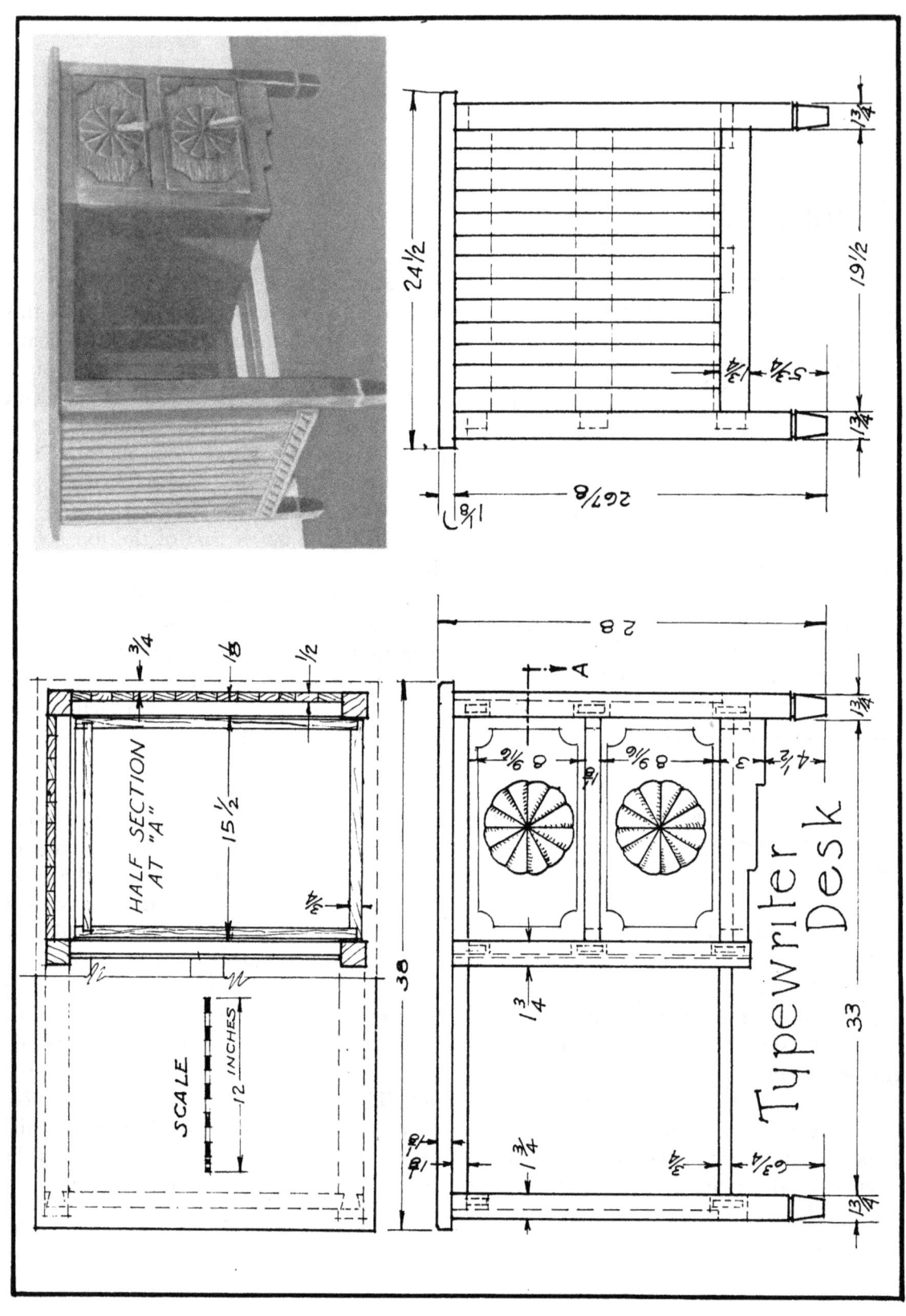

Typewriter Desk

BILL OF MATERIAL

Pieces		
4	1¾ by 1¾ by 26⅞	Legs
2	1¾ by 1¾ by 21½	Uprights
2	¾ by 4 by 35	Lower stretchers
6	1⅛ by 2½ by 21½	Crosspieces
2	1¾ by 2 by 21½	Lower crosspiece ends
2	¾ by 8 9/16 by 15½	Drawer fronts
4	¾ by 8½ by 20½	Drawer sides
2	¾ by 8⅜ by 14½	Drawer backs
1	¾ by 3 by 15½	Apron
4	1⅛ by 2 by 21½	Drawer supports
2	1⅛ by 1¾ by 35	Upper stretchers
20	½ by 2 by 19⅜	End panels
16	½ by 2 by 21	Back panels
1	¼ by 19½ by 21½	Center panel
2	¼ by 14½ by 20½	Drawer bottoms
1	1⅛ by 24½ by 38	Top

While this desk might be slightly out of place in the living room of a home, it would be found appropriate in a schoolroom or a den where the tables and chairs are Spanish colonial. The girl student would like it for her room, and it might help the boy to concentrate more readily on his work. A shelf could be placed in the opening of the desk for a typewriter when not in use.

CONSTRUCTION

The two ends are constructed separately with crosspieces at top and bottom. The center section is made the same as the ends, but with the legs cut off. Blind mortise-and-tenon joints are used. The three sections are tied together by stretchers at the top and the bottom. These stretchers are notched into the crosspieces and are held in place with 2-inch screws. Frames are made for the drawer supports. They are notched for the legs and are held in place with screws. This construction holds the frame rigid. The covering for the two ends and the back is composed of ½-inch material, 2 inches wide. These pieces can be beveled on the two outside edges to give a V-shaped groove where they come together. This is characteristic of the early pieces of furniture. These pieces are scraped lengthwise with the sharp teeth of a small backsaw to give them a pitted finish. They are nailed in place with 1¼-inch No. 18 brads. The top is made of 1⅛-inch material and extends over the sides and ends about ¾ inch. The top edges should be rounded slightly.

CARVING

The regular potassium dichromate finish is used. The directions for carving the rosette are given in the special chapter on carving. The lower crosspieces on the ends can be carved with a series of parallelograms, and these can be rounded into a roped design by taking off the corners with a chisel or a knife. The edges of the top can also be carved.

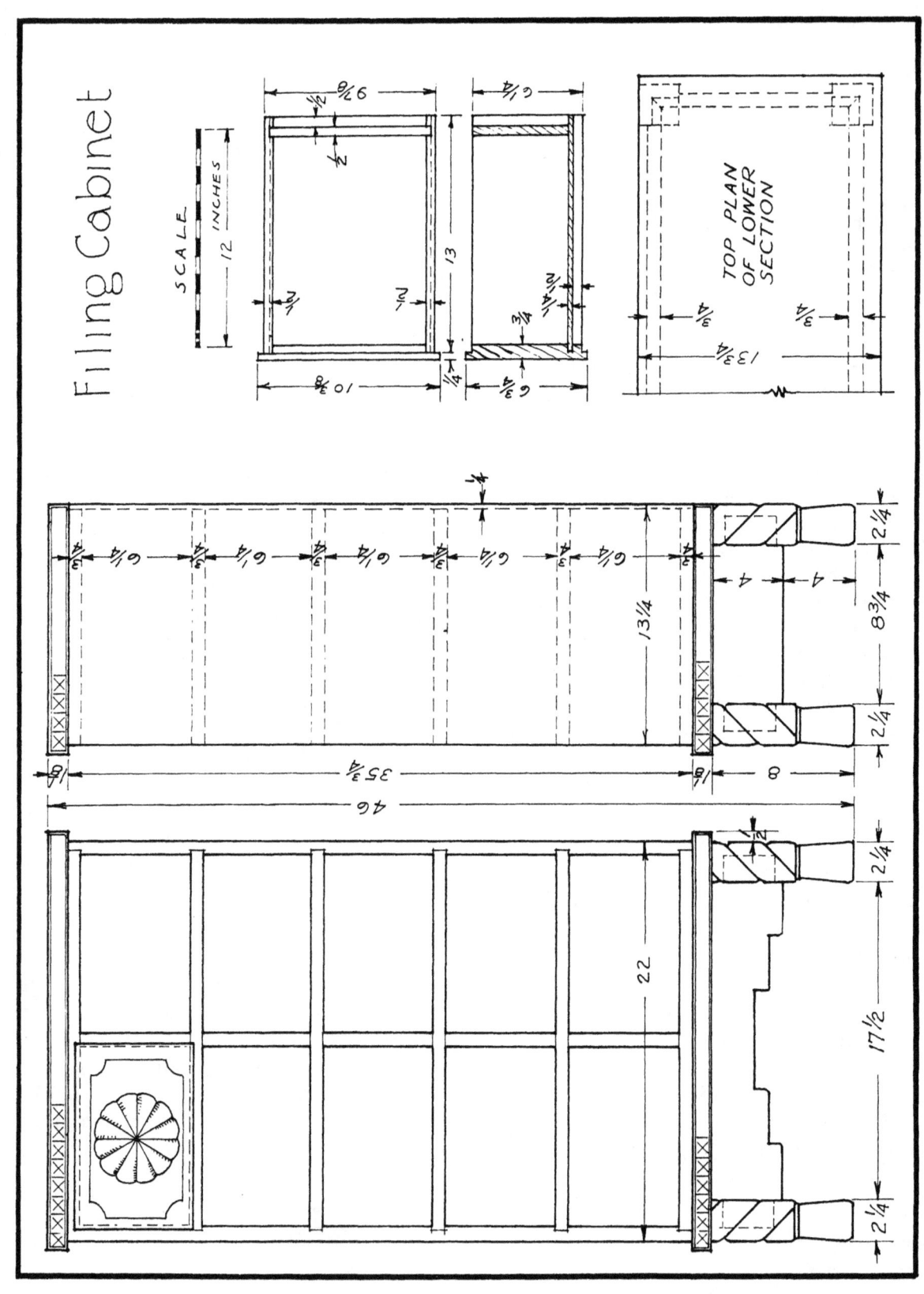

Filing Cabinet

BILL OF MATERIAL

Pieces

BOTTOM SECTION

4	2¼ by 2¼ by 8	Legs
2	¾ by 4 by 20½	Side rails
2	¾ by 4 by 11¾	End rails
1	1⅛ by 13¾ by 23	Top

TOP SECTION

2	¾ by 13¼ by 35¾	Ends
6	¾ by 13 by 21	Frames, outside dimensions
5	¾ by 6¼ by 13	Drawer separators
10	¾ by 6¾ by 10⅜	Drawer fronts
20	½ by 6¼ by 13	Drawer sides
10	½ by 5½ by 9⅜	Drawer backs
10	¼ by 9⅜ by 13	Drawer bottoms
1	1⅛ by 13¾ by 23	Top
10	1 by 1 by 2½	Drawer pulls
1	¼ by 21 by 35¾	Back

A piece of furniture of this type apparently has little use in the home. The original article illustrated was made for an art room where the other furnishings were Spanish colonial. However, the same cabinet, with a different arrangement of drawers, makes an attractive piece of furniture for the study or den.

CONSTRUCTION

The construction is similar to that of the high chest described elsewhere. The sides are cut to size and grooved to take the drawer supports as well as the top and bottom crosspieces. The drawer supports are frames built up, by notching the drawer separators to take the end supports. The frames are nailed from the ends so that no nailheads show when the parts are assembled. These frame supports can be grooved ⅛ by ¾ inch to take the center drawer separators. A solid piece can be used for these center separators, or frames can be constructed to fit.

CARVING

The decorative scheme is conservative and is fixed by the general style adopted. The rosette fits the surface to be decorated. The drop pulls enrich the scheme and give it a distinction. It is something more than a cheap, pine filing cabinet.

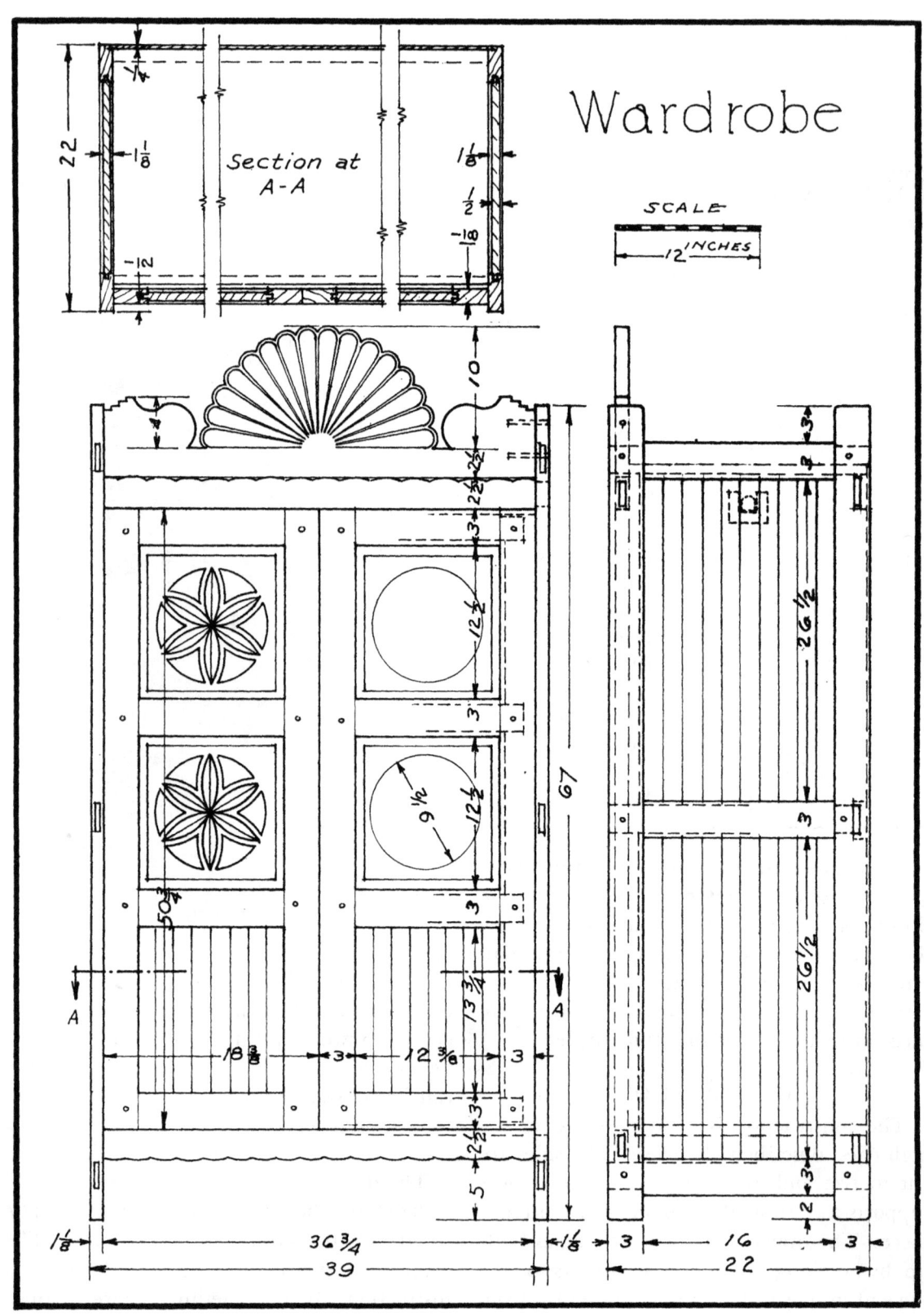

Wardrobe

BILL OF MATERIAL

Pieces		
4	1⅛ by 3 by 67	Posts
6	1⅛ by 3 by 22	End rails
40	½ by 1 11/16 by 27	End panels
5	1½ by 2½ by 39	Crosspieces
1	1⅛ by 12½ by 36¾	Headpiece
1	¼ by 37¼ by 56	Back
	DOORS	
4	1⅛ by 3 by 50¾	Stiles
8	1⅛ by 3 by 16⅜	Rails
4	¾ by 12⅞ by 13	Upper panels
16	½ by 1⅝ by 14¼	Lower panels
2	1⅛ by 20 by 36¾	Top and bottom
4	hinges, decorative	

The Spanish colonists had but few luxuries. Undoubtedly the wardrobe was considered as such, for it was not generally found in the early homes. In both French and Spanish homes the wardrobe was considered a necessity, but the colonists had very little surplus clothing to hang in a wardrobe.

The ancient adobe home, built around a patio, had but very little closet space. The partitions were often of adobe, and consequently could not be arranged to allow for small closet spaces. Wardrobes became a necessity under such conditions.

CONSTRUCTION

The two ends are built as a unit. The posts and crosspieces are grooved to take the panel material, and each is glued up and secured with pins. Next, the four crosspieces, front and back, tie the ends into position by the through mortise-and-tenon joints. The backpieces are grooved to take the back panel. The top and bottom rests on these and on cleats fastened to the ends.

The doors are assembled as shown in the plate. Decorative hinges will add to the attractiveness of the doors.

The carved headpiece is held in place with dowel pins.

The lower parts of the doors and the ends are paneled with ½ by 9/16-inch strips beveled on both outside edges.

CARVING

The half rosette on the headpiece has the concave type of carving as shown in the illustration. The door panels have six-point designs made with the compass. The panel material is scraped lengthwise with a sharp backsaw, sanded lightly, and finished with the regular finishing solution. The hinges can be handmade. Those shown in the illustration were cut to shape with a hack saw.

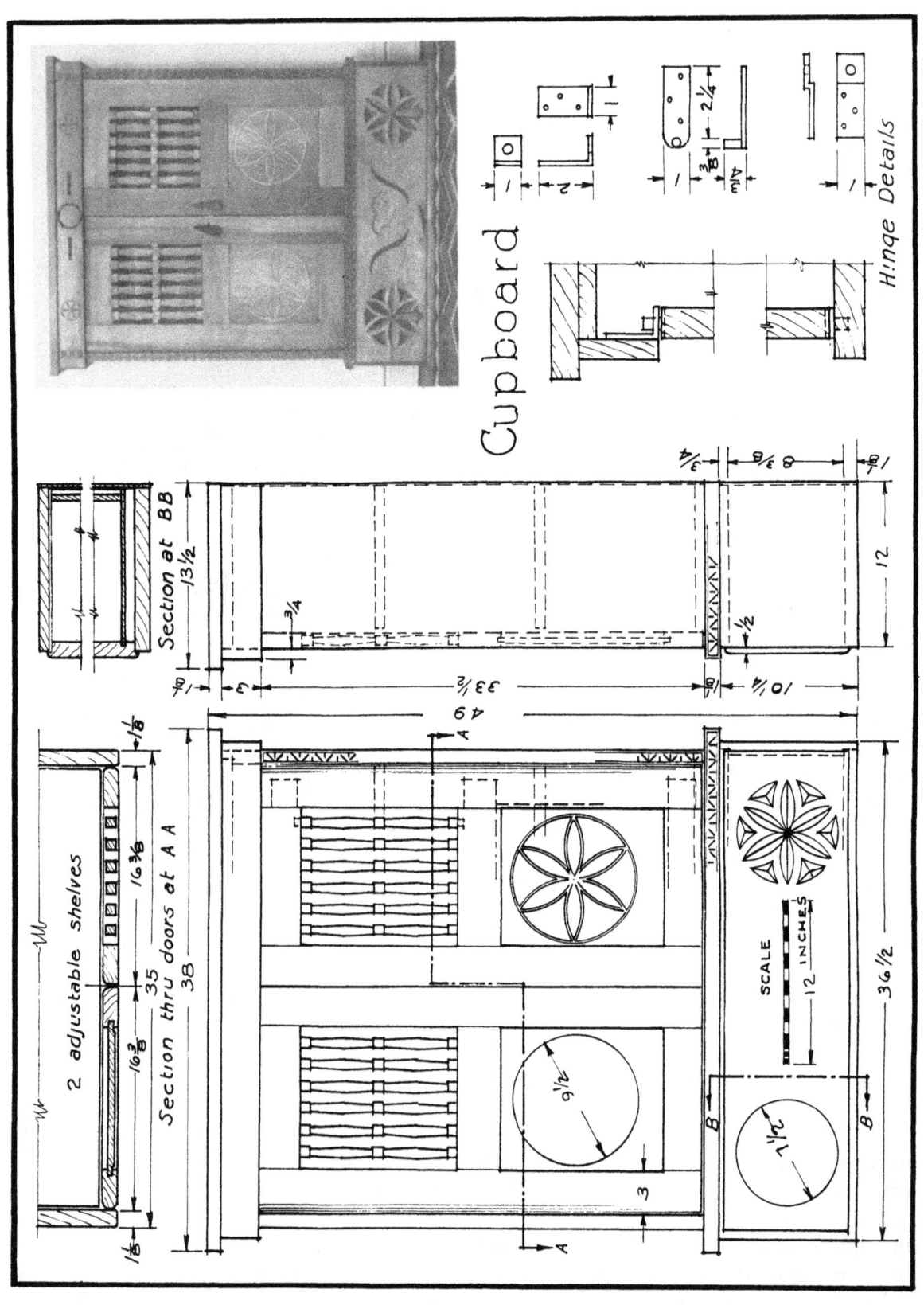

Cupboard

BILL OF MATERIAL

Pieces

UPPER UNIT

1	1⅛ by 13½ by 38	Top
1	¾ by 11¾ by 33¾	Piece under top
1	¾ by 3 by 36½	Front apron
2	¾ by 3 by 12¾	Side apron
2	1⅛ by 12 by 36½	Sides
1	¼ by 33¼ by 36½	Back
1	¾ by 10⅝ by 33¾	Bottom
2	¾ by 10⅜ by 32¾	Shelves

DOORS

4	1⅛ by 3 by 33½	Stiles
6	1⅛ by 3 by 14⅜	Top, center, and bottom rails
12	1 by 1 by 13¼	Laths
2	½ by 10⅞ by 12¾	Panels
	Hinges (see detailed drawing)	

LOWER UNIT

1	1⅛ by 12¾ by 38	Top
1	¾ by 11¾ by 35¼	Piece under top
1	1⅛ by 11¾ by 35¼	Bottom
1	¼ by 10¼ by 34¾	Back
2	1⅛ by 12 by 10¼	Sides

DRAWER

1	1⅛ by 9¼ by 35	Front
1	¼ by 11¼ by 33½	Bottom
1	½ by 7½ by 33½	Back
2	½ by 8 by 11½	Sides

The cupboard here shown is smaller than the usual cabinet of this type. It was made to serve a particular need, that of a storage place for dishes and table linen, and it can be used in a small dining room in place of a buffet. It is not deep, so it takes up but little space.

CONSTRUCTION

The cupboard is built in two units, as are other cabinets of this type. The lower unit is a boxlike structure housing the one drawer. The upper unit has two crosspieces notched to the lower ends as well as the upper ends of the two sides. Screws through the lower pieces hold the two units together and the doors in place.

In the old Spanish colonial pieces, the doors swung on dowel rods. The top and bottom corners were reinforced with strap iron to keep the dowels from splitting the wood. It is better to follow the hinge details shown in the plate or to buy regular hidden hinges. By removing the screws that hold the two units together, the top is tilted back and the doors can be removed at will. The doors must be rounded to allow them to swing freely. The facing around the top is built as a unit of the toppiece, and the whole is held in place by screws through the top crosspiece from the inside. This will allow for expansion. The shelves are held in place by cleats screwed to the sides, or can be made adjustable by using regular hardware for that purpose.

CARVING

The illustration and plate show the details of the carving. The carving on the door panels is not very deep; that on the drawer is heavier. The center design above the doors is decorated with blue and red paint, which is a typical Spanish colonial feature. To execute the design, two concentric circles are described; the space between the circles is laid off in ½-inch segments, and chips are cut out. The two colors of paint are applied to alternate segments. The chip carving on either side of the central figure is decorated in a similar manner.

Cupboard

BILL OF MATERIAL

Pieces

BOTTOM SECTION

2	1⅛ by 18 by 21⅜	Ends
1	1⅛ by 19 by 44	Top
3	1⅛ by 17¾ by 40½	Shelves
2	1⅛ by 9½ by 40½	Drawer fronts
4	¾ by 9 by 17½	Drawer sides
2	¾ by 8⅜ by 38⅝	Drawer backs
2	¼ by 17½ by 38⅝	Drawer bottoms
1	¼ by 21⅜ by 40½	Back panel

TOP SECTION

2	1⅛ by 14 by 44⅞	Ends
1	1⅛ by 15 by 40½	Top
4	1⅛ by 3 by 40⅜	Door stiles
6	1⅛ by 3 by 17	Door rails
4	1⅛ by 12⅝ by 37	Shelves
1	¾ by 4½ by 40	Facing, front
2	¾ by 4½ by 14¾	Facing, ends
1	¼ by 36¾ by 44⅞	Back panel
2	¾ by 12⅝ by 15½	Door panels
14	1⅛ by 1⅛ by 17⅜	Door grille
2	Metal plates, ⅛ inch thick, to support doors	
4	⅝ by 4 Dowel rods	
3	Feet of molding	

This particular type of cupboard has found favor with owners of Spanish-type homes. It usually is placed in the dining room, but could be used in a hallway or on a sleeping porch. It makes a good storage cabinet in a dormitory or a schoolroom. It is rather imposing, evincing an atmosphere of dignity and charm.

CONSTRUCTION

The construction is similar to the wall cabinet described on page 129. The drawer space is not so large, and the whole piece is not as deep as the first one described. The size depends upon the purpose for which it is to be used and upon the size of the room. It is built in two sections and fastened together with screws. By loosening the screws, the top tilts back and the doors drop out.

The cabinet can also be taken apart to move it. Flat hidden hinges can be used instead of the dowels. Handmade wrought-iron hinges will add to the attractiveness. The grillwork on the top sections of the doors is not difficult. Cut ½-inch tenons on each end of the pieces before carving, and then bevel the edges to give the desired shape to the face. The bottom panels are planed on the face to fit grooves in the doors, thus making the surface convex.

CARVING

The carving is rather intricate and somewhat difficult. The various forms of the rosette are laid out with a compass. The illustration shows the details better than they could be explained in writing. Other forms could be substituted. The chip carving calls for careful work. The knife should be sharp. Practice on a piece of scrap wood until the right pressure on the knife is learned. A skew chisel works very well on this job. The interlacing of the lines across the facing at the top, carried across both ends, is not difficult. The lines are laid out freehand and are shaded to show the portion to be carved. After

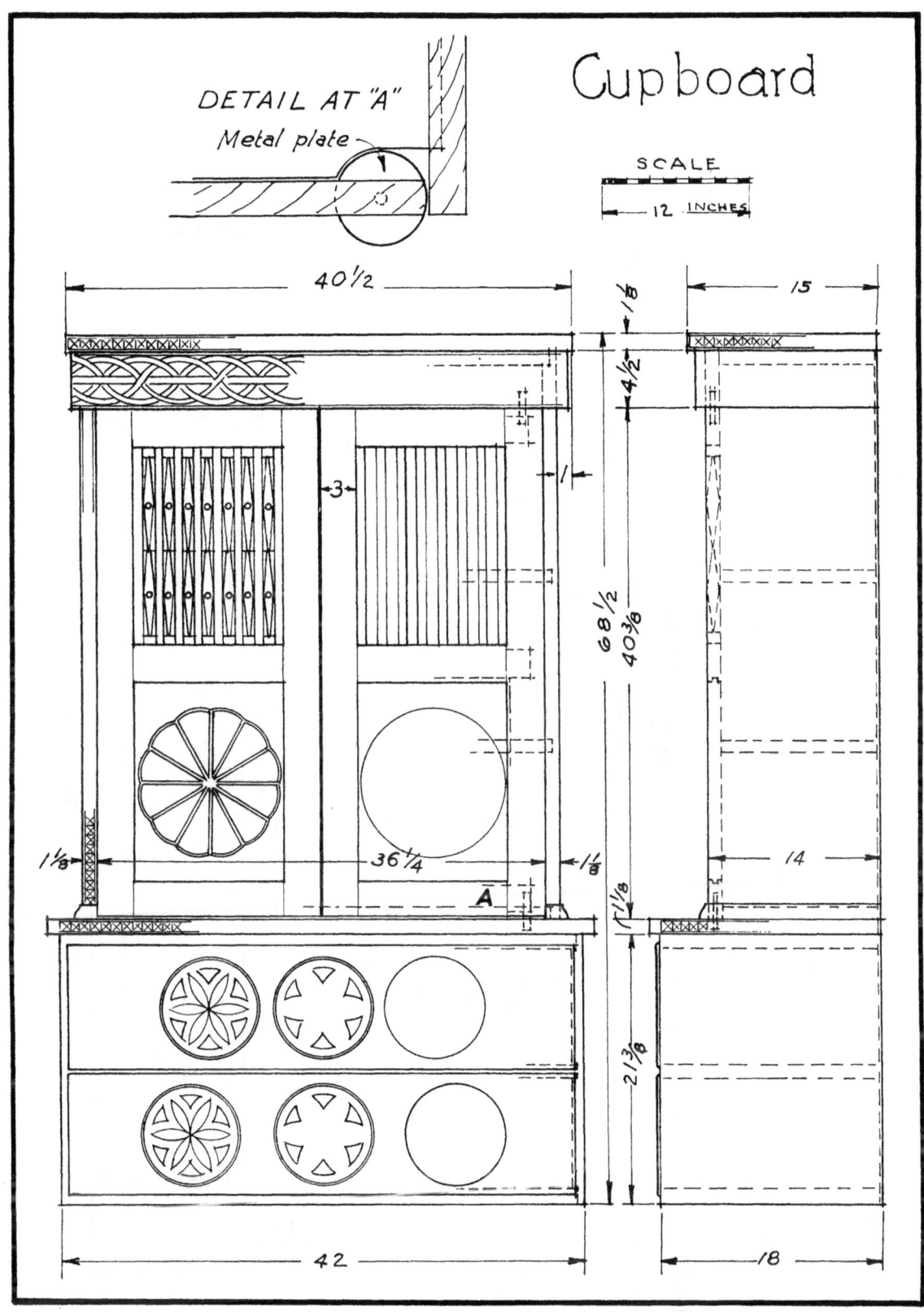

the lines have been run with the sharp point of a knife, the low places are carved out to the depth of ⅛ inch with a small gouge. The rosettes on the door panel are carved to a depth of ⅛ inch. The spaces between the lines are about ½ inch wide and are rounded with a knife or chisel. All edges are beveled and sanded.

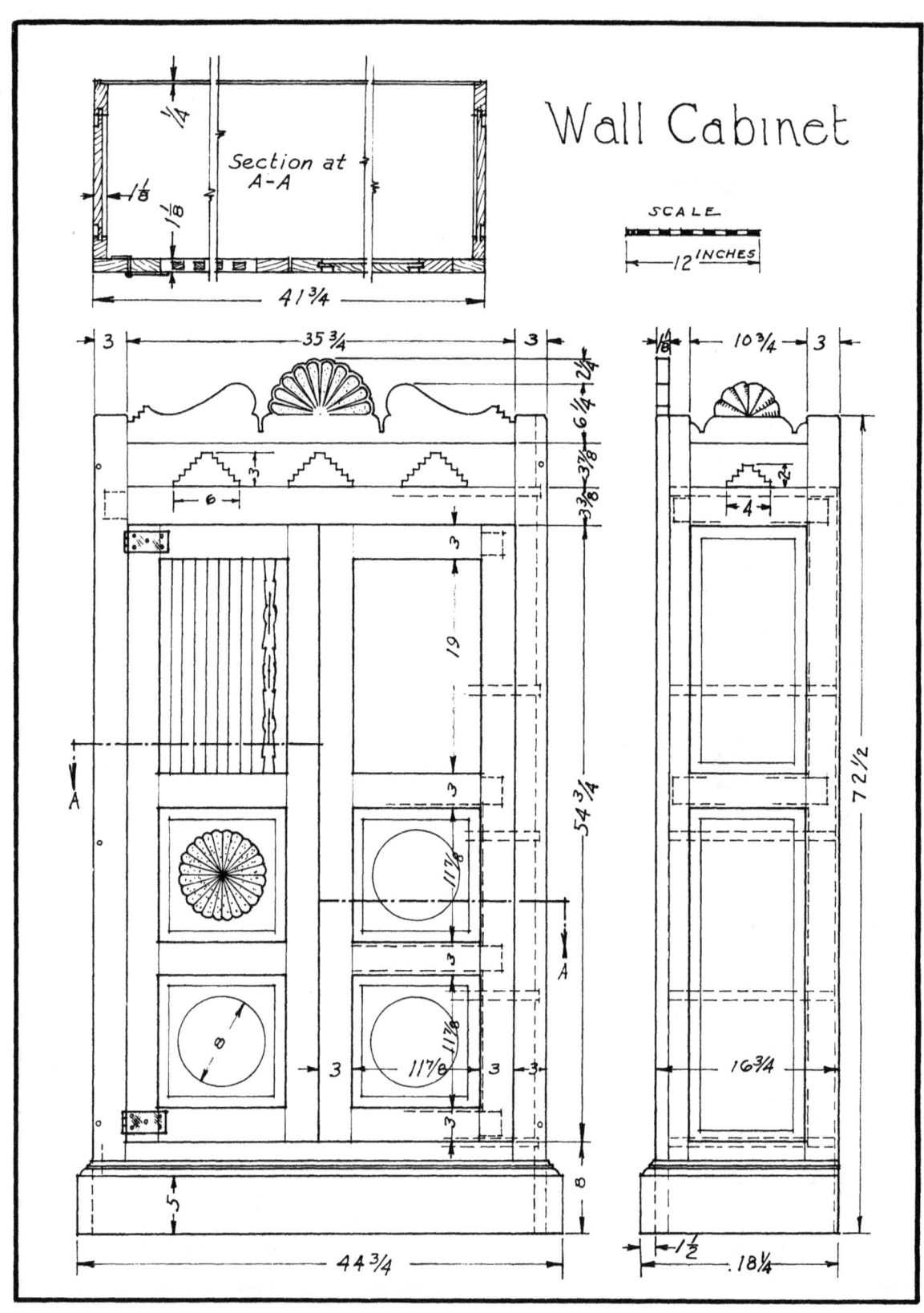

Wall Cabinet

BILL OF MATERIAL

Pieces

END UNITS

2	1⅛ by 3 by 72½	Back posts
2	1⅛ by 1⅞ by 72½	Front posts
6	1⅛ by 3 by 14¼	Cross rails
2	¾ by 11¼ by 30¼	Lower panels
2	¾ by 11¼ by 22½	Upper panels
2	1⅛ by 3⅞ by 10¾	Upper decorations
2	1⅛ by 6¼ by 10¾	Upper decorations
5	¾ by 15 by 40	Shelves
1	¼ by 40 by 66½	Back

FRONT

4	1⅛ by 3 by 54¾	Door stiles
8	1⅛ by 3 by 15⅞	Door rails
4	¾ by 12⅜ by 12⅜	Door panels
10	1⅛ by 1¼ by 20	Door grille
1	1⅛ by 3⅞ by 35¾	Front decoration
1	1⅛ by 8½ by 35¾	Front decoration
2	1⅛ by 3 by 72½	Posts

FACING

2	¾ by 5 by 18¼	Ends
1	¾ by 5 by 44¾	Front
7		Feet molding

HINGES

The hinges should be handmade of ⅛ by 2-inch material

The trastero or wall cabinet is part of the furnishing of every Spanish-type home. This particular style of cabinet can be used either as a cupboard in the kitchen or, if made without the shelves, as a wardrobe in the bedroom or on the sleeping porch. It carries the atmosphere of the Spanish colonial period.

CONSTRUCTION

The two ends are built as units and are glued up with the panels in place. The front is built as a unit with the doors in position as indicated in the plate. Then the front is secured to the ends with countersunk screws, and the holes are filled with dowel pins to cover the heads of the screws. Square pieces cover the tops of the corners as imitation posts. The decorative headpiece is secured with dowel rods. The doors swing on dowel pins or hinges if desired. In the old pieces the corners were often reinforced with strap

This old wall cabinet with turned stiles and rosette design in the pediment provided inspiration for the present wall cabinet

iron. The facing on the apron is secured in position by the use of screws from the inside of the posts. Cleats are used to hold the shelving in position. If used as a wardrobe, the back should be solid to brace the structure.

CARVING

The designs are characteristic of the early carving. The outlines are cut to a depth of about ⅛ inch. The figures are hammered with a dull instrument. The lattice front on the door is a true Spanish colonial feature. The strap-iron reinforced hinges on the doors are typical of the work of the earlier craftsmen. This cabinet must have an environment of adobe walls and riprap ceiling.

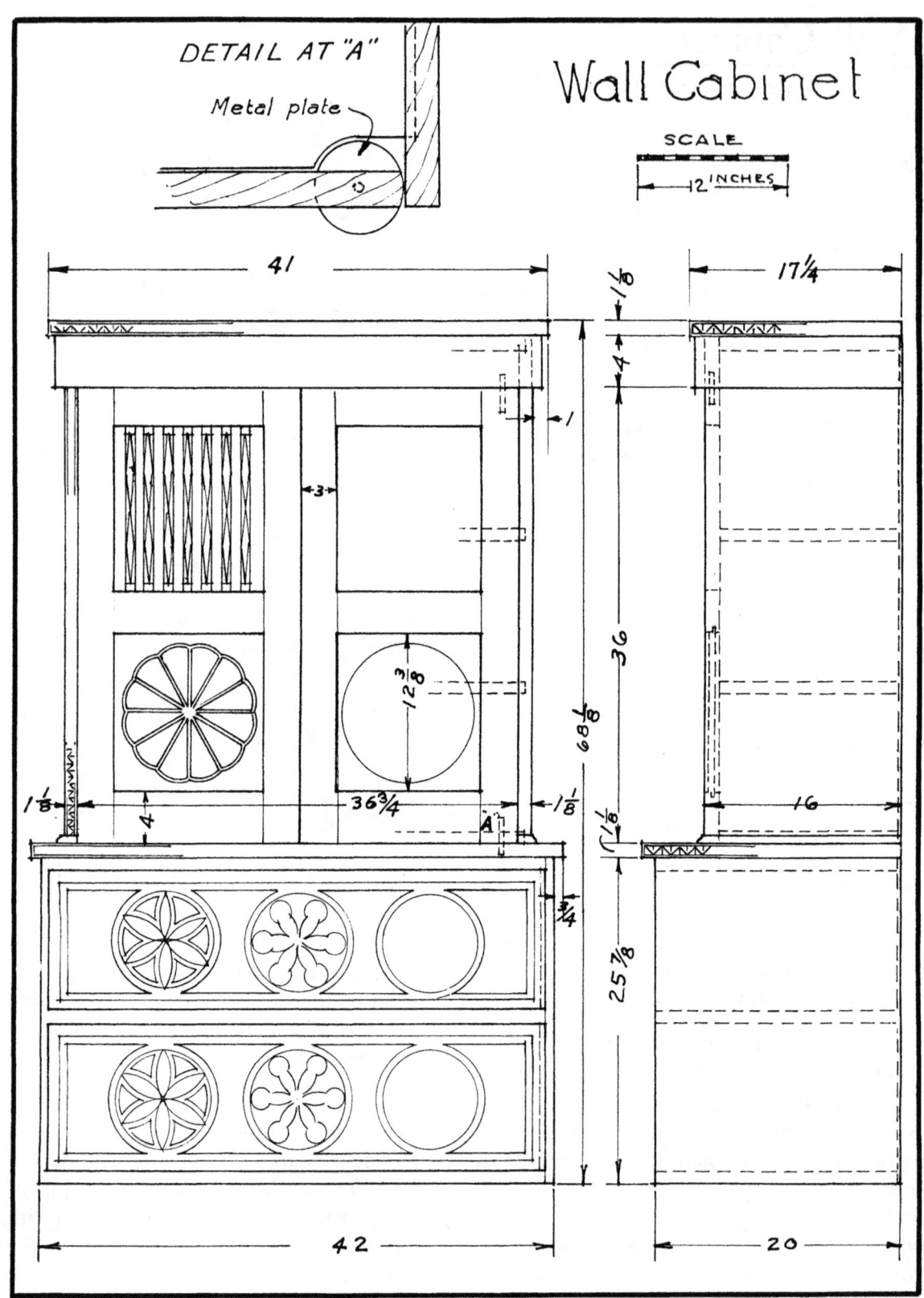

Wall Cabinet

BILL OF MATERIAL

Pieces

BOTTOM SECTION

2	1⅛ by 20 by 25⅞	Ends
3	1⅛ by 19¾ by 40½	Shelves
2	1⅛ by 11¼ by 40½	Drawer fronts
4	¾ by 11⅛ by 19	Drawer ends
2	¾ by 10½ by 38⅞	Drawer backs
2	¼ by 19 by 39⅜	Drawer bottoms
1	1⅛ by 20¾ by 43½	Top
1	¼ by 40½ by 25⅞	Back

TOP SECTION

2	1⅛ by 16 by 40	Ends
4	1⅛ by 15¾ by 37½	Shelves
4	1⅛ by 3 by 36	Door stiles
4	1⅛ by 3 by 16⅜	Door rails (top and middle)
2	1⅛ by 4 by 16⅜	Door rails (bottom)
2	¾ by 12⅞ by 12⅞	Door panels
14	1⅛ by 1⅛ by 14½	Door grilles
1	¾ by 4 by 40½	Facing, front
2	¾ by 4 by 16¾	Facing, ends
1	1⅛ by 17¼ by 41	Top
1	¼ by 37½ by 40	Back
4	⅝ by 4	Dowel rods
2	Metal plates for doors	
3	Feet of molding	

The kitchen and dining room of a Spanish colonial house were not complete without a trastero or wall cabinet. In the modern Spanish home trasteros are found in the bedroom and on the sleeping porch as well. They are rugged reminders of the colonial period.

CONSTRUCTION

These cupboards are built in two sections; the lower boxlike structure holds two drawers. The upper portion is built as a unit with shelves, and the two crosspieces are notched into the top and bottom of the sides. The plate shows these crosspieces as one solid piece the same as the shelves. This will take a little more material, but it makes a stronger structure. This unit is fastened to the bottom unit by screws going through these crosspieces. The doors are swung on dowel rods, the bottom rods fitting into the lower unit. By loosening the screws, the top section is tilted back and the doors can be put in place or removed at will.

CARVING

The designs are mostly variations of the rosette. The doors in the cabinet shown are characteristic of the older cabinets. The latticework usually was similar to this. The facing across the top, not shown in the plate, is the daydream of a Navajo carver and is as unrelated as some of the patterns of Navajo rugs, but it is well balanced and distinctive.

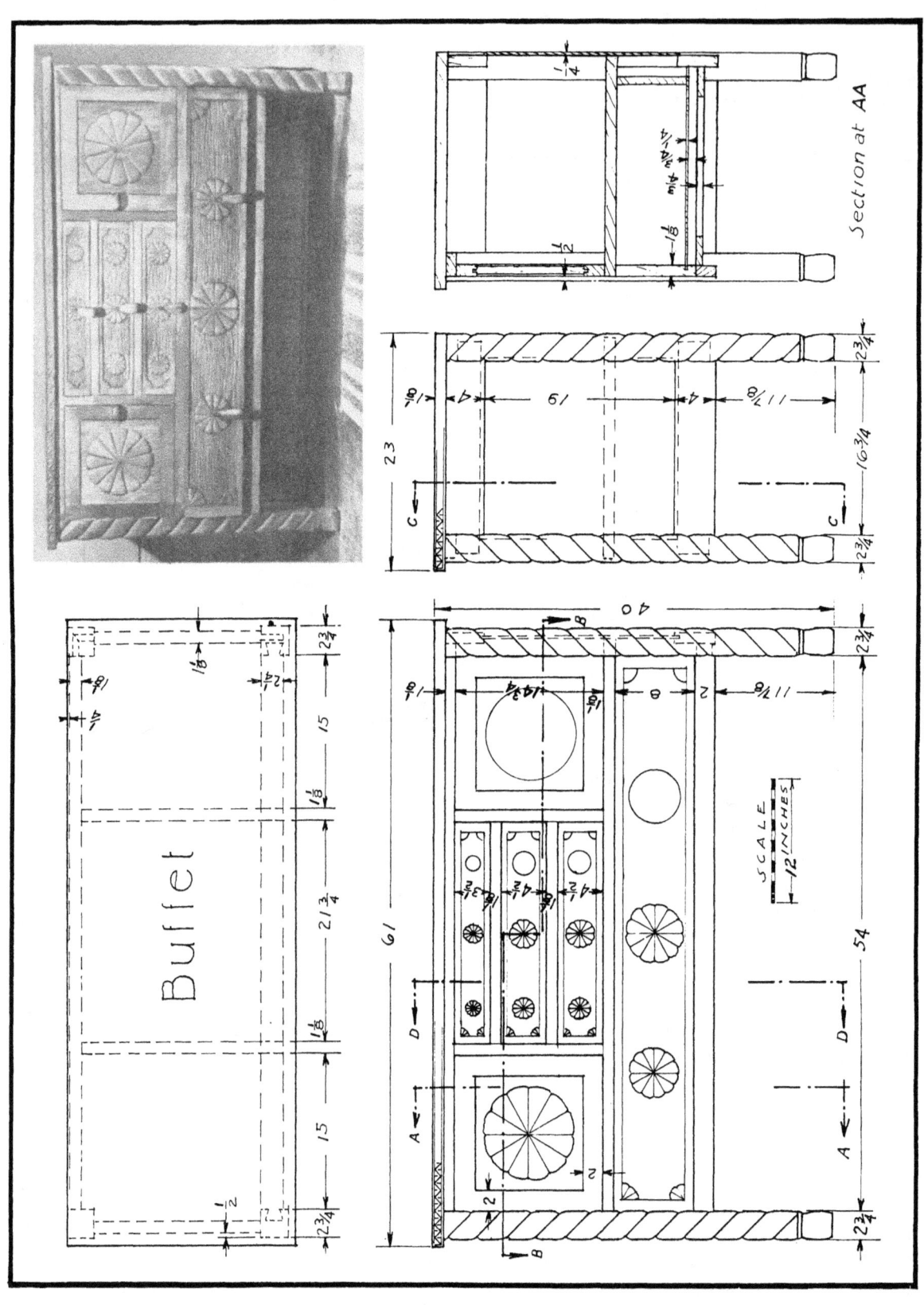

130

Buffet

BILL OF MATERIAL

Pieces		
4	2¾ by 2¾ by 38⅞	Legs
1	1⅛ by 2¼ by 56½	Front upper stretcher
1	1⅛ by 21½ by 56½	Middle separator
1	1⅛ by 2 by 56½	Front lower stretcher
2	1⅛ by 4 by 57½	Back rails
4	1⅛ by 4 by 20¼	End rails
2	¼ by 17¼ by 19½	End panels
1	¼ by 19½ by 54½	Back panel
2	1⅛ by 14¾ by 21½	Inside upright panels
4	1⅛ by 2 by 14¾	Door stiles
4	1⅛ by 2 by 15	Door top and bottom rails
2	¾ by 11½ by 11¼	Door panels
4	1⅛ by 3 by 21¾	Rails for drawer support frames
4	1⅛ by 3 by 19½	Rails for drawer support frames
2	¾ by 3 by 17¼	Rails for drawer support frames
2	¾ by 3 by 56½	Rails for drawer support frames
2	1⅛ by 1⅛ by 16¾	Drawer guides
2	1⅛ by 4½ by 21¾	Drawer fronts
1	1⅛ by 3½ by 21¾	Drawer front
4	¾ by 4½ by 22	Drawer sides
2	¾ by 3½ by 22	Drawer sides
2	¾ by 3¾ by 21	Drawer backs
1	¾ by 2¾ by 21	Drawer back
3	¼ by 21 by 22	Drawer bottoms
1	1⅛ by 8 by 54	Drawer front
2	¾ by 8 by 22	Drawer sides
1	¾ by 7 by 53¼	Drawer back
1	¼ by 22 by 53¼	Drawer bottom

This particular type of buffet fits in well with a dining-room table having twisted iron braces, and chairs with spiral pieces in the back. The set usually includes the table, seven straight chairs, an armchair, and the buffet. If the room is large, a carved chest with a drop lid and ornamental hinges is placed in one end of the room, and a corner shelf might contain pieces of Pueblo pottery. The floor should have two or three Navajo rugs. The drapes should be of monk's cloth, a natural gray, decorated with Pueblo embroidery. The dimensions given for this buffet should be followed rather closely, as they give balance and proportion.

CONSTRUCTION

The legs are cut from 2¾ by 2¾-inch squares. The spirals are cut on two sides only, following directions as given in the chapter on cutting spirals. That portion of the legs below the apron is carved on all sides. The apron cannot be widened unless it is cut away in the center. The drawer separators are all 1⅛-inch stock, as are the doors, drawer ends, and top. The top could be 1⅜-inch material. The drop pulls are 1⅛ by 1⅛ by 3 inches, and the turns for the doors are 1⅛ by 1⅛ by 2 inches. The top rail is dovetailed in the tops of the front legs, otherwise mortise-and-tenon joints are used throughout. The uprights between the doors and drawers are grooved on the corners to take the panels. Similar uprights in the back are notched to fit the two upper rails which are similar to those in the front. The legs should be grooved to take the end panels. The 2-inch screws holding the turns on the doors have a piece of 16-gauge metal brazed on the heads, so when the knob is turned the metal fits into a groove in the upright.

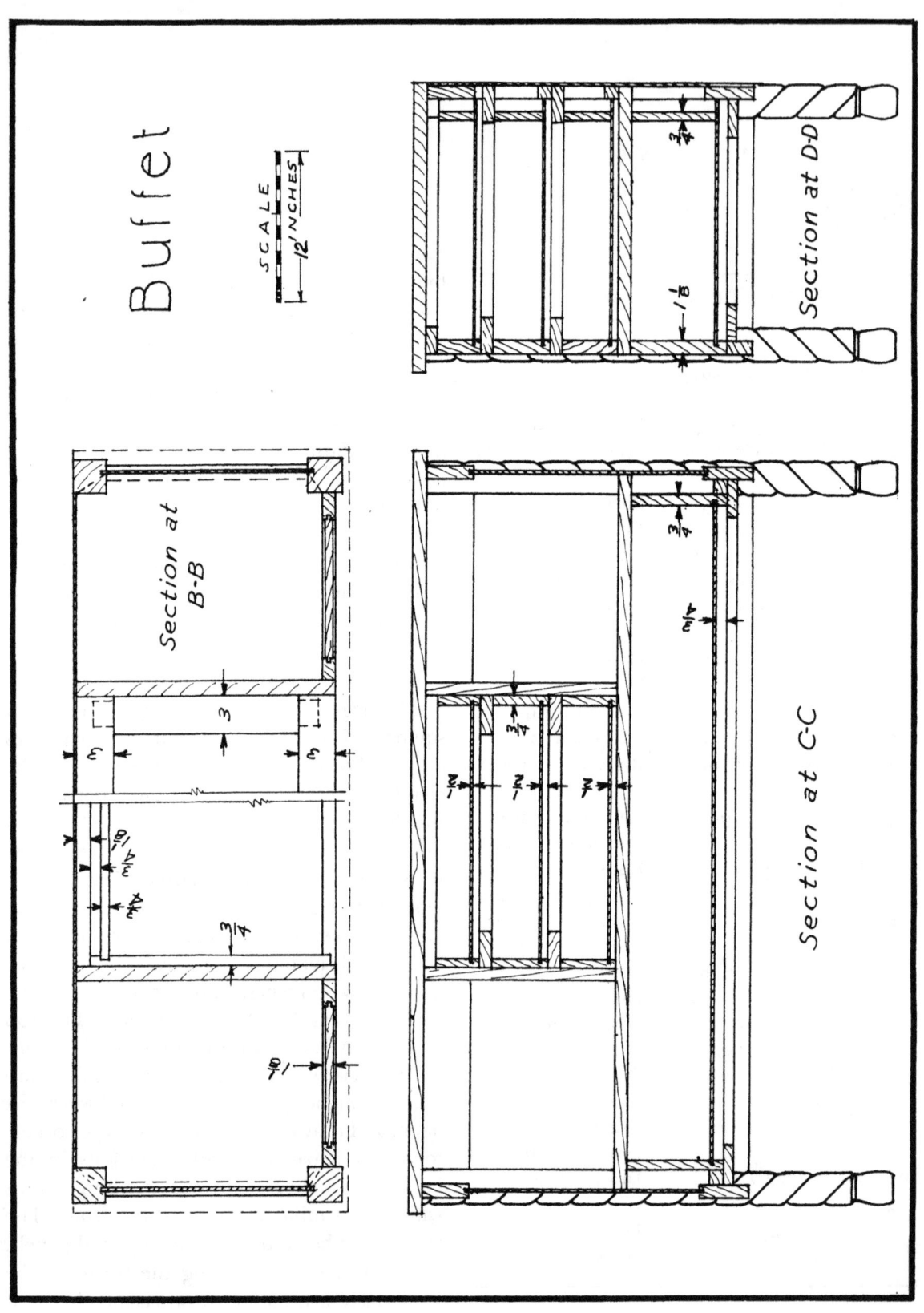

132

CARVING

The designs are simple and easily done. The center row of rosettes could be omitted, and two drop pulls could be placed on each of the three top drawers. The corner decorations on the long drawer could be smaller. It would possibly add to the appearance if the hinges were of hammered wrought iron.

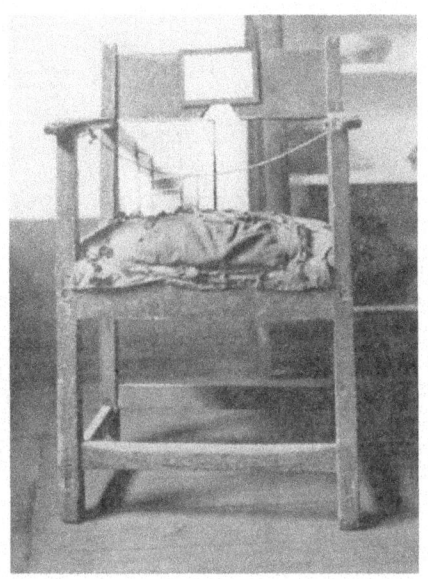

An old Spanish chair in
a New Mexico museum

Index

Antiques, Spanish colonial, 1-7
Armchair, 38, 39, 40, 41, 42, 43; Spanish, 34, 35, 36, 37

Bed, double, 96, 97; twin, 94, 95
Bedside table, 56, 57
Bench, fireplace, 74, 75, 76, 77; patio, 78, 79, 80, 81
Bookcase, open, 26, 27, 28, 29; sentinel, 24, 25
Box, wood, 82, 83
Braces, iron, 14, 62, 66
Buffet, 130, 131, 132, 133
Bullet design, 13, 48, 86

Cabinet, filing, 118, 119; wall, 126, 127, 128, 129
Carved grille, 122
Carving, chip, 12, 13; edge, 12, 13; feet, 12; panels, 8, 9; rosette, 8; spiral legs, 10, 11
Chair, dining, 30, 31, 32, 33
Chest, 86, 87, 110, 111; early Spanish, 84, 85; Spanish colonial, 88, 89
Chest of drawers, 108, 109
Chip-carving designs, 13
Coffee table, 44, 45
Console table, 52, 53
Cupboard, 122, 123, 124, 125

Design, and construction, 1; elements of, 4
Desk, small, 105, 106, 107; typewriter, 116, 117; writing, 114, 115
Dictionary stand, 90, 91, 92, 93
Dining chair, 30, 31, 32, 33
Dining table, 60, 61, 62, 63
Double bed, 96, 97
Dovetailed joints, 85
Drawer knobs, 57
Drawer pulls, 14
Dressing table, 112, 113
Drop pulls, 14

Edge carving, 12, 13
End table, 46, 47, 48, 49, 50, 51

Feet, layout of, 12
Filing cabinet, 118, 119
Finish, 14
Fir for table legs, 51
Fireplace bench, 74, 75, 76, 77
Fluting, 37, 43

Grille, carved, 122; roped, 30, 40, 76

Hall tree, 22, 23

Hasps, 14, 84
Highboy, 98, 99; Spanish, 100, 101
Hinges, 14, 85

Leather, commercial, 43
Legs, roped, 10, 11; spiral, 10
Library table, 64, 65, 66, 67
Living-room table, 58, 59
Locks, 14
Lowboy, Spanish, 102, 103, 104

Magazine table, 72, 73
Meander design, 13, 66

Nails, ornamental, 43

Occasional table, 68, 69
Open bookcase, 26, 27

Paint used in design, 123
Patio bench, 78, 79, 80, 81
Potassium dichromate used as water stain, 15

Rawhide for seat, 43
Roped design, 13
Roped facing, 27
Roped grille, 30, 40, 76
Roped legs, 10, 11
Rosette, concave or convex, 8, 9; elliptical and round, 8; layout and carving, 8; panels, 8, 9; round and diamond-shaped, 9

Sentinel bookcase, 24, 25
Serving tray, 16, 17
Shellac on table tops, 15
Small desk, 105, 106, 107
Smoking stand, 18, 19, 70, 71
Spanish armchair, 34, 35, 36, 37
Spanish colonial chest, 88, 89
Spanish highboy, 100, 101
Spanish lowboy, 102, 103, 104
Spiral legs, 10
Square table, 54, 55
Step-up design, 32, 53, 72, 78
Stool, 112, 113
Stretcher, wedged, 64

Table, bedside, 56, 57; coffee, 44, 45; console, 52, 53; dining, 60, 61, 62, 63; dressing, 112, 113; end, 46, 47, 48, 49, 50, 51; library, 64, 65, 66, 67; living room, 58, 59; magazine, 72, 73; occasional, 68, 69; square, 54, 55
Table-top fasteners, 61, 65, 67

Template, 35
Tile table top, 45
Tray, serving, 16, 17
Triangle design, 13
Twin beds, 94, 95
Twisted iron braces, 14, 62, 66
Typewriter desk, 116, 117

Wall cabinet, 126, 127, 128, 129
Wardrobe, 120, 121
Wastepaper box, 20, 21
Wood box, 82, 83
Writing desk, 114, 115

www.ingramcontent.com/pod-product-compliance
Lightning Source LLC
Chambersburg PA
CBHW050501110426
42742CB00018B/3335